'In his book *Mindful Business Leadership*, Robbie has created an easy to use matrix with nine unique archetypes guiding you through the skills of being a leader. I especially like Robbie's idea of the Conductor, a mindful personal advisor offering guidance to use the right archetype at the right time. Not naturally mindful? Don't worry – Robbie has got you covered with many different techniques you can practice.'

**Dominic Lynch**, Learning and Development Manager, Central London Hotels, Marriott International

'Insightful, exciting and transformational on many levels. Steinhouse's Leadership Matrix takes us on an extraordinary journey to help unlock true leadership potential.'

**Eva Hamilton** MBE, Founder and CEO, Key4life

'Robbie Steinhouse is a rare breed: a leadership expert who actually is an experienced business leader.'

**Frank Pennal**, Chief Executive Officer, Property/Banking Division, Close Brothers Group PLC

'Robbie Steinhouse's *Mindful Business Leadership* could do for business leadership what Steven Covey's *Seven Habits* did for personal development. Steinhouse is a highly successful entrepreneur and business leader. He is also a world authority on NLP. In this book he combines real-world business know-how with deep insight into what makes business leaders tick. The result is an important book for anyone who wants to do better at building and leading a business.

*Mindful Business Leadership* clearly explains the ten elements of leadership in the Leadership Matrix Model. It describes instantly recognisable archetypes and their shadows, and explores how these archetypes can be used to develop a more flexible and effective leadership style. The second half of the book provides detailed practical exercises and guides for how to apply the Leadership Matrix personally to become a more successful and engaging leader.

Steinhouse is an expert at taking complex ideas and presenting them in a clear and accessible way, without diminishing their power. With personal anecdotes, wide-ranging references, meticulous research and its author's mastery of psychology, *Mindful Business Leadership* is a rich new resource that will help anyone who wants to improve their leadership in business and beyond.'

**Francis Currie**, Content Director, Wireless Group – including Virgin Radio, talkSPORT and talkRADIO

'This strikes me as an excellent book, written with intelligence, clarity and eloquence, combining cutting-edge ideas with timeless wisdom and plain, old common sense. It draws on the author's wealth of experience both as a coach

D1613341

and as a businessman. It will be of use to leaders in all fields seeking to deepen their understanding of the role and overcome hidden barriers to success.'

**Jose Zalabardo**, Professor, Head of Department,
Department of Philosophy, UCL

'*Mindful Business Leadership* by Robbie Steinhouse draws on a lot of experience and knowledge of the subject and offers us a new model, using archetypes as a way to understand ourselves better as leaders and bring more balance, awareness and presence, not only in the context of leading but also in the context of life. This is a wonderful and useful book, so needed in the world of organisations and business. The world will greatly benefit from the learning here.'

**Judith DeLozier**, NLP founding member, Creator of Six Step Reframing and Somatic Syntax, Co-author of *Encyclopaedia of NLP*

'Robbie is that unusual combination of a successful business person and a philosopher. He has not only succeeded, but has asked, at a deep level, *how* he has done so. His answers are always insightful, often surprising and never dull.'

**Mike Southon**, Author of *The Beermat Entrepreneur*

'As an experienced business leader, it isn't often I am surprised by a business publication, but Robbie Steinhouse has achieved this here. The simplicity of the models allowed me to step back and reflect on my own style and self-awareness. As a result, I have rebalanced archetypes, which is helping me to be a more effective leader. First class! I would recommend this book to any business leader.'

**Mark Cliff**, Chairman and CEO, The Brightside Group

'*Mindful Business Leadership* offers a unique and important look at leadership – viewing the multiple roles that are required to be effective in business, and offering mindfulness as a crucial way to keep all of the roles balanced. Here, the nine roles that leaders play are made memorable by connecting each with an archetype. Here too, Robert calls for a mindful balance by pointing out the shadow side of each and how leadership can go wrong. The book ends with many practical exercises for mindfulness.'

**L. Michael Hall**, PhD, Author of *Unleashing Leadership* and *Collaborative Leadership*

'*Mindful Business Leadership* is a clear and insightful guide to improving your performance as a business leader by focusing on the things that matter. The Leadership Matrix Model is particularly powerful in developing understanding of successful leadership.'

**Noel McGonigle**, HR Director, UK and Europe, Savills

'The new book by Robbie offers a practical guide to business acumen *for* business leaders *from* a business leader. It is sharp, fun to read and concise. The matrix of leadership roles is just brilliant. Overall, the book is an excellent development tool and an aide-memoire for any aspiring or seasoned business leader.'

**Nikoloz Shurgaia**, CEO, Nikoil Bank

'This is another great book from Robbie, and one that anyone in business, whether currently working as an employee, manager, director or coach, will come back to time and time again. It's an excellent manual for developing your business leadership skills, for combining your intuition and business acumen, while being thoughtful, centred and avoiding burning out. Highly recommended.'

**Phil Parker**, Designer of the Lightning Process

'This book combines many of the principles of the Hoffman Process: that we are made up of different, quite separate parts, and that with the power of mindful intent we can bring them to the fore to serve us best.'

**Serena Gordon**, Managing Director and Co-founder, Hoffman UK

'Robbie Steinhouse speaks from experience about the roles a leader needs to step into. You can't wait for "winter" to arrive to learn the multiple ways of thinking, acting and being that a leader needs to master. This book will guide you through the process, so that you can succeed at leading an organization, whatever the season.'

**Shelle Rose Charvet**, Author of *Words That Change Minds* and *The Customer Is Bothering Me*

'*Mindful Business Leadership* is a brilliant yet eminently practical book. Robbie Steinhouse wonderfully describes how effective leadership requires mastering different roles, each having its important counterpart, and each having both positive and negative forms. The most important skill is thus the mindfulness to balance and nimbly craft these complementary skills into a creative matrix. I found the book exceptionally helpful to both my personal and professional development, and I believe you will too.'

**Stephen Gilligan**, PhD, Psychologist and Author of *The Hero's Journey*

'The model in this book is an ideal framework for thinking about the various aspects of leadership that can be applied in different circumstances. Robbie presented this at a previous Trust's leadership conference and got very positive feedback from health service leaders.'

**Sue Sjuve**, Chair, Royal Surrey County Hospital NHS Foundation Trust

'As a senior leader you can focus all of your time and energy on your objectives, but forget to step back to gain perspective. The leadership course I attended under Robbie's tutelage allowed us to step back from the day to day and, with collegiate feedback, helped raise our awareness and hone our personal leadership skills.'

**Talbot A. Stark**, CFA, Global Head of Institutional Sales, BNP PARIBAS Global Markets

'Far from being only conceptual, *Mindful Business Leadership* provides enlightening keys which have been shaped by Robbie Steinhouse's personal experience and deep understanding of management behaviour. Whether you are a beginner or already advanced in your career, whether you want to start a journey towards leadership or because you are simply curious, this book will help you put words to many situations of your professional and personal life. This book will talk to you.'

**Xavier Domec**, Senior Corporate Development Officer, BNP Paribas

'With *Mindful Business Leadership,* Robbie Steinhouse presents a thought-provoking, instructional guide to those wishing to improve their leadership abilities through good old-fashioned self-study, reflection and skills development. In his commitment to explore the question of what makes a great business leader, Steinhouse draws from his own experience as a business leader and professional coach – including years of continuing education, observation of and discussion with leaders from various environments and disciplined study.

*Mindful Business Leadership* approaches effective leadership as a combination of genuine and thoughtful vision, character and deliberate development and balance of essential leadership traits or "capability sets". Steinhouse walks the reader through a logical and accessible matrix model of leadership with down-to-earth, practical advice, real-life examples and metaphors and genuine encouragement and enthusiasm. As the title implies, the approach that Steinhouse outlines, emphasises and encourages the importance of mindfulness in the important, day-to-day work leaders carry out.

I greatly enjoyed and highly recommend *Mindful Business Leadership* as a valuable resource for leaders of all types and at all stages of their careers.'

**Tracey Armstrong**, President and CEO, Copyright Clearance Center

'This book calls on giving thought to business leadership at a number of levels, be it for talent, coaches or leaders themselves. It is a reference book I recommend keeping on your desk or even your nightstand, to consult whenever you wish to think before you act.'

**Yvon Doukhan**, Head of Senior Management Training BNP Paribas, (Previously Director, Secretary General of Arval and Member of Executive Committee – BNP Paribas Group)

'Robbie's latest book manages to achieve what many other leadership books fail to do: interweave psychology with organisational design, practical application with deep philosophical insights. The imagery, stories, metaphors and personal experiences add to the rich texture of the book and leave the reader with a clear roadmap for leadership and its application, both as a personal journey and as a highly practical business strategy. I have seen the benefits of the book on our Masters students who have now almost spontaneously developed a new language, frequently using terms like 'Boss', 'Compass' and 'Fox' from the model. The Leadership Matrix is highly accessible and intuitive, and I am convinced that this book will create a popular movement for adopting leadership more widely.'

**Paul Sternberg**, Associate Dean, Head of Design Innovation, Ravensbourne

'Robbie is like Alan Sugar meets the Dalai Lama! More seriously, this book provides a practical way for the twenty-first century leader to develop the diverse range of skills needed for success.'

**Julian Russell**, Managing Director, PPD Consulting

'Robbie Steinhouse has succeeded in providing business leaders with a unique and practical model to address day-to-day leadership challenges in his book, *Mindful Business Leadership*. It is excellent reference material for any leader or aspiring leader, highlighting the importance of making space for reflection and awareness of both self and the immediate environment, in order to achieve business and personal success.'

**Brendan Collins**, HR Director, Mazars LLP

'Robbie once again offers an in-depth and comprehensive investigation into leadership, based on vast life experience. He brilliantly applies well-known NLP processes to business situations. Excellent diagrams complement and enhance the text, which will help the individual transform their leadership style, harnessing their 'shadow' qualities. Powerful analogies make reading and application of the text easy.

The workbooks on mindfulness and mission and vision help to centre the reader, and a 'meaty' appendices section adds psychological depth.

A highly recommended read for leaders of any sector – corporate, charity, services, entrepreneurs and students of life.'

**Dr Ann-Marie Wilson**, BCA Executive Director of 28 Too Many

# Mindful Business Leadership

*Mindful Business Leadership* presents a new model of leadership. It introduces ten very different leadership roles that are required to meet the challenges of modern business. Memorable metaphors and images are created for each, and they are placed in a matrix. Readers are told how to develop these roles within themselves. Potentially negative aspects of each are discussed, along with material on how to put these to creative use. The book argues that mindfulness is the best way to balance the roles – a mindful leader will know 'who to be' in any situation. The last part is taken up with clear, practical exercises that readers can practice to become more fully mindful and develop a clear vision for their own leadership.

*Mindful Business Leadership* is relevant to anyone, anywhere in the world, who is moving (or wishes to move) to a position of leadership.

**Robbie Steinhouse** has many years' experience of business leadership, coaching and NLP training. He is Chairman of Gray's Inn Group, the property and insurance businesses he founded in 1987. He is an ICF certified coach and managing director of the Coaching Consultancy. He is a certified NLPU and ANLP Master NLP Trainer and head of training at NLP School in London. As an executive coach, leadership and NLP trainer, he has worked with numerous clients across the world in business, government and the third sector including Accenture, BNP Paribas, Bank of England, BBC, Coca Cola, Disney Corp, HSBC, KPMG, NHS, Rolls Royce, Tesco, Vodafone, the UN and the Red Cross. Robbie is the author of *Think Like an Entrepreneur*, *Brilliant Decision Making*, *How to Coach with NLP* and *Making Effective Decisions*, which have been translated into seven foreign language editions.

# Mindful Business Leadership

**Robbie Steinhouse**

*Robbie Steinhouse* (signature)

Routledge
Taylor & Francis Group

LONDON AND NEW YORK

First published 2018
by Routledge
2 Park Square, Milton Park, Abingdon, Oxon OX14 4RN

and by Routledge
711 Third Avenue, New York, NY 10017

*Routledge is an imprint of the Taylor & Francis Group, an informa business*

© 2018 Robbie Steinhouse

The right of Robbie Steinhouse to be identified as author of this work
has been asserted by him in accordance with sections 77 and 78 of the
Copyright, Designs and Patents Act 1988.

All rights reserved. No part of this book may be reprinted or reproduced or
utilised in any form or by any electronic, mechanical, or other means, now
known or hereafter invented, including photocopying and recording, or in
any information storage or retrieval system, without permission in writing
from the publishers.

*Trademark notice*: Product or corporate names may be trademarks or
registered trademarks, and are used only for identification and explanation
without intent to infringe.

*British Library Cataloguing-in-Publication Data*
A catalogue record for this book is available from the British Library

*Library of Congress Cataloging-in-Publication Data*
A catalog record for this book has been requested

ISBN: 978-1-138-30110-8 (hbk)
ISBN: 978-1-138-30111-5 (pbk)
ISBN: 978-0-203-73277-9 (ebk)

Typeset in Bembo
by Deanta Global Publishing Services, Chennai, India

MIX
Paper from
responsible sources
FSC
www.fsc.org   FSC™ C013985

Printed in the United Kingdom
by Henry Ling Limited

I dedicate this book to my wife, Anna Steinhouse –
leadership is fundamentally about following your heart,
and I am so happy to lead my life with her.

# Contents

**PART IV**
**Mission and vision workbook**                                    **91**


**PART V**
**Appendices**                                                     **97**

# Acknowledgements

First, I want to thank my wife Anna for her feedback, engagement and help throughout the writing process. Her own leadership experience working in the banking sector has proved invaluable.I want to thank Kristina Abbotts at Routledge for commissioning this book and making the entire process elegant, pleasant and professional. I would also like to thank Georg Wanek at Taylor & Francis for his introduction and encouragement.

I would like to thank my long-term writing coach and editor, Chris West, for painstakingly making suggestions to tighten up the model, text and the book's overall structure – we share a passion that books should be both succinct and enjoyable to read. I would also like to thank our artistic wizard, Justin Swarbrick of What Communications, for creating all the images and diagrams in this book.

This book has also been greatly influenced by my having worked with various clients, especially having taught for the past decade on the global leadership programmes for École Polytechnique in Paris. Thanks also to my numerous coaching clients for trusting to share their journey with me. They helped open my eyes to challenges in different business sectors which enabled me to broaden this book beyond my own experience.

I also want to thank Yuki and Akane Horiguchi, who encouraged me to develop a business model and invited me to teach it several times in Tokyo. I have presented the Matrix model internationally in the United States, Russia, China and around Europe. This helped me understand that these archetypes have universal characteristics.

I wish to thank my many teachers. First, Robert Dilts, whose ability to structure immensely complex ideas into simple and useable models has been truly remarkable. Stephen Gilligan's Three Minds and Archetype model and Judith Delozier's NLP process based on the work of Carol Pearson have also been an inspiration. I would like to thank Brendan Collins of Mazars for introducing me to various leadership models, including TA. I also want to thank Paul Sternberg for inspiring me and showing that it is possible to live a life based on a vision beyond conventional success. A special thank you to Stephen

Covey and Hyrum Smith for their amazing contribution to this field. Other teachers I have mentioned throughout the text.

Finally, I would like to thank the amazing team of people who have worked with me at Gray's Inn Group for so many years; there are too many to list here, but I would like to especially thank the leadership team and fellow directors Jenny Jackson, Michael Hayman and Darren Pither (and Gillian Dow, now retired) and the dozens of staff who have worked there over the years. They helped me build a business and I hope they also feel they have shared in its success. I would also like to thank the many customers, suppliers and financiers who have trusted and stuck by us.

I would really like to hear your comments on this book. Please email me at robbie@leadershipmatrix.com or visit www.leadershipmatrix.com.

# Preface

It is a particular pleasure to write this preface for Robbie Steinhouse's new book *Mindful Business Leadership*. Robbie and I have been colleagues and friends for many years. Not surprisingly, we have many common interests, including a deep passion for NLP, entrepreneurship, coaching and leadership. Robbie weaves all of these powerful resources together in his fascinating and informative new work.

In *Mindful Business Leadership*, Robbie presents his intriguing and entertaining *Leadership Matrix*. He identifies *mindfulness* – a wise and witnessing self-awareness – which functions as a 'conductor' for the elements in the Matrix.

Robbie's emphasis on mindfulness stresses one of the unique and important contributions he makes to the world of business – the intimate relationship between personal and professional growth. A key premise of my own Success Factor Modelling work is that, in order to grow our professional career or venture, we must also grow and evolve personally. The mindset that brought us to where we are today will not take us to the next stage. *Mindful Business Leadership* is a powerful resource to help you make this progress.

As with his other books, Robbie's writing style is friendly, lucid, direct and practical. He provides many personal experiences, practical examples and exercises, which demonstrate how the various elements and principles he presents may be developed and applied to support your own evolution as a leader, creating a solid bridge between knowing and doing.

Robbie is an excellent teacher and trainer, as evidenced by the fact that he is both an affiliate and an on-site trainer for my NLP University in Santa Cruz, California. His understanding of leadership is clearly enhanced, enriched and given credibility by the fact that he has applied what he is teaching to his own life and business.

As an author of several books on leadership myself, I can attest that *Mindful Business Leadership* is a great practical guide to becoming a better and more effective leader. Robbie Steinhouse's integration of enhanced mindset and mindfulness is a winning approach!

Robert B. Dilts
NLP developer and creator of the Logical Levels (Leadership Pyramid), Hero's Journey and Disney Process; author of over 20 books, including *Strategies of Genius* and the forthcoming *Conscious Leadership*.

# Introduction

The question of what makes a great business leader has fascinated me for years. I am a leader myself – though I must admit that I didn't set out to be one. I started my niche property business back in 1987 more with the intention of having longer holidays rather than of becoming a leader. The business has since grown into one of largest in the sector. Leadership is something I've found myself having to learn – initially by doing and later by study.

I am also a coach, and have run leadership programs and worked directly with many leaders in organisations of differing sizes, helping them work through all kinds of issues connected with leadership and its challenges.

This has led me to study numerous approaches to leadership over the years, but a while ago I decided to develop my own model. I wanted to find a way of combining the intellectual rigour of business psychology with the seasoned experience of the commercial world. I set myself this target: 'real business with a learnable structure'.

I began by talking to leaders who impressed me: coaching clients, customers, colleagues, friends – if they had 'walked the walk', I wanted a little bit of their time to ask them what they thought was the secret.

Perhaps the most revealing of these conversations was with John. If there is a stereotype of a leader, it is of someone charismatic and larger-than-life. John, by contrast, is a shy, introverted man. However, he not only built a large manufacturing business from scratch, but has managed to survive the vast array of market changes over the past 30 years. My dad, who was also an entrepreneur, often said, 'It's easy to make money; it's difficult to keep it'.

I didn't expect a romantic view of leadership from John, and I didn't get one. Instead, I got a reply that lingered in my mind, one that kept coming back to me when others made grander claims. He simply said:

> The difference between me and the directors in my business is that each of them (finance, sales, purchasing, operations, human resources (HR) etc.) is better at their jobs than me. However, I could do any of their jobs and none of them could do each other's. I am better than average at all the key functions of business.

He went on to say:

> Your success is determined not by how good you are at one of these functions, but by how bad you are at one thing – your Achilles Heel if you will. The area in which you have *not* gained at least moderate competence will be your downfall.

And added:

> If you don't understand these core functions sufficiently well, then your directors will try and get things around you simply because it is easier for them to do so. To put it bluntly – unless you know what you are doing, they will try and bullshit you. This wider knowledge is therefore essential to gain your directors' respect and for them to trust your judgement. You have the wider perspective; allowing them to become the 'power behind the throne' can be very dangerous. They must share all important information with you and seek your counsel on any significant decision. You always have the right to be given the final call on your business.

These words chimed with my experience. On occasions, my finance director will look at me in a certain way, and I am pretty sure that he's saying to himself, 'Do I have to tell him this?' After a resigned sigh, he will then tell me whatever it is. We then have a discussion, after which I am quite happy to go with his view if he can explain why. If I wasn't competent at finance and attuned to how finance people think and feel, I would not be able to do this.

I found John's approach very illuminating, but I still felt something was missing.

Another person I talked to was a consultant called Sarah, who was passionate about leadership development. 'Leaders', she told me, 'build great teams and develop other leaders'. She also said, 'There isn't a simple leadership "mould". It is essential for each leader to develop themselves to become a better, but still authentic, version of themselves'.

Other interviewees talked about vision and the importance of both having it in the first place and keeping hold of it when times get tough. They talked of the ability to generously share a vision, beyond charisma, and to create a culture that transcended their own personality.

I couldn't buy totally into John's model of someone who simply had (nearly) the abilities of all their top people. Leaders have to do – and be – other things, too. New things, that they hadn't had to do or be before they accepted the calling of leadership, like developing talent or holding vision. John, I feel, did these new things well, but didn't realise it. One of the many discoveries I made from my discussions is that people often have only partial insight into what they do and how they do it. But what are these things, exactly?

Another topic that has fascinated me for a long time is personal development – taking ownership of our continuing education and using that learning to transform our lives. That began in 1995 when my father had a heart attack. Up until then, I had been focused on building my business and not really been reflecting on myself (or the deep psychology of others). But this event made me step back and ponder the bigger picture. I received coaching, which led me to get very into neuro linguistic programming (NLP) and then transactional analysis (TA) (see Appendix B). In 2000, I started parallel careers as a coach myself and as an NLP trainer. Surprisingly, as I spent more time focusing on these skills and delegated the core functions of my business, the business grew much faster than I could have possibly imagined. I would never have achieved the level of success that I have done had I remained an unreflecting, controlling manager/owner.

The first idea that influenced my leadership model came from my teachers of NLP, Robert Dilts, Judith Delozier and Stephen Gilligan. It is that of *archetypes*, inspired by the classic works of Carl Jung. In essence, this concept models the human personality as a cast of characters. Each one of these sub-personalities has its own sense of the world and its place and role within it. Each one feels particular emotions strongly – and can also be oblivious to certain other emotions. Each has its own energy. Archetypes aren't passive things. They're not little boxes to put thoughts and feelings into; they are forcefully striving to express themselves, to make themselves real in the world out there – including, of course, the world of business.

Archetypes have *shadows*. I will discuss these in more detail in later chapters, but for now I just need to say that there are potentially destructive qualities associated with archetypes' essentially positive energies. Determination, for example, can shade over into obsessiveness. Yet these, too, can be helpful to us: our shadows can also reveal our weaknesses and the parts of us we disown, and thereby act as a powerful catalyst for change. It is also worth noting that the brighter an archetype shines, the greater the shadow it casts.

A second concept that I discovered on my personal development journey, and which proved essential to my leadership model, was that of *mindfulness*. It struck me that while the leader needs to have a range of archetypal sub-personalities at their disposal, these are not much use if not deployed in the right place at the right time. Leaders need to be able to rise above the strong feelings of the moment and decide wisely which energies to connect to, which versions of themselves to be. Mindfulness gives that detached perspective.

In an orchestra, the conductor mindfully stands back and enables the appropriate instruments to perform at their best at the right time. Mindfulness is our inner conductor, with the instruments being our diverse archetypes or business abilities. I recently saw a movie about the life of Steve Jobs, and was delighted to see this principle acted out. In a scene that takes place in a concert hall, Steve Jobs shares a metaphor with Apple cofounder, Steve Wozniak. Wozniak is like a great musician, a section leader such as the first violin. Jobs is the conductor, who doesn't play an instrument; he says, 'I play the orchestra'.

Over time, I worked on various ways of combining and presenting the various archetypal sub-personalities that the business leader needs to have at their disposal – the exact list of instruments in the conductor's orchestra. In the end, I produced the matrix below.

| Conductor | Vision | Character | |
|---|---|---|---|
| | | Yang | Yin |
| Leadership | Compass | Boss | Coach |
| Operations & Finance | Architect | Express train | Alarm bell |
| Sales & Marketing | Radar | Fox | Friend |

Welcome to my model, the 'Leadership Matrix'. At first glance, some parts may seem obvious, others puzzling and a few problematic. I will enjoy explaining it to you in depth in the pages that follow. I hope it will become your guide for lasting leadership success.

**Part I**

# Nine elements of leadership

# 1   Vision and character (yang and yin)

This part of the book is about the nine archetypes inside the main 'box' of the Leadership Matrix (the Matrix). But first, I want to look at the two axes and explain why they are as they are. I shall start with the horizontal axis.

| Conductor | Vision | Character | |
|---|---|---|---|
| | | Yang | Yin |
| Leadership | Compass | Boss | Coach |
| Operations & Finance | Architect | Express train | Alarm bell |
| Sales & Marketing | Radar | Fox | Friend |

## Vision

This book seeks to breathe new life into the concept of *vision*. Leadership requires a genuine focus on vision and creativity – ever more so, as the business world changes more and more rapidly.

At the same time, vision must not be just an ethereal activity. It is there to create clear benefits: a positive culture, a unique market position and identity and the ability to continuously create new products and services (or adapt existing ones). There is also a 'mechanistic' vision – of a business run with elegant processes. And vision cannot just be insular; it needs to extend outside the organisation to form a wider world view.

This book also argues that different business functions have their own unique visions. Finance directors see the world differently to sales directors. Both see a bigger picture, but a different bigger picture. Far from generating chaos, the tension between these various visions can be highly creative.

Vision is desirable from the moment you start to take on direct reports. If you start your career journey by only spotting what others do wrong, you will not develop the essential skills needed later, when you are asked to lead a larger unit. This is the reason, I believe, why the person who can run a ten-person business or department often can't run a 100-person unit, or the person who can run a 100-person unit stumbles at running one with 1,000 people (and so on). People who hit these career ceilings lack the ability to evolve a vision, both for themselves and for their people. Instead, you have to grow with the challenge: as Jack Welch said, 'If the rate of change on the outside exceeds the rate of change on the inside, the end is near'.

This means creating a bespoke vision for the team you lead, one that is genuinely inspirational. Creating a vision at this level is not just a regurgitation of the corporate mission – it is active work, and I have seen how good team leaders use this skill to help harmonise a vision between their team and that of the larger organisation.

The bigger the challenges faced by the leader, the more essential vision becomes. I coached Keith, who was the managing partner of a successful mid-size professional partnership but was now struggling after a major acquisition. His solution was to work harder, but he was burning out: he told me once, 'I don't work that hard. I never get to the office before 5.30am'. His approach to business was to fix things that weren't working, but this no longer seemed sufficient. A big breakthrough came when he suddenly looked at me and said, 'I don't know where I am going'. This was a powerful insight for me, too. Keith had worked out that the next phase of his evolution into leadership was to develop a clear vision for where both he and the partnership were headed. He needed to shift from micro-managing partners to trusting them to lead their function under a guiding vision.

Vision is also something that needs flexibility, the ability to 'zoom in and out', to see a grand vision but also to see if it is relevant to a specific individual in the team. One also needs to be able to consider the vision from different timeframes, to adjust and make a vision more robust by anticipating potential problems. These are all within the skill set of visioning.

## Character

True excellence in any area of business is not just about knowing how to do things, it is about being the right kind of person for the job. It is about having the right *character*.

Character is a term that can have a wide variety of meanings. Beyond personality, it is about having a set of values and then living by them – having personal integrity. It is also something that has to be worked on: people can be born with talent, but character requires effort to develop and maintain, especially under pressure.

Character is not something people either have or don't have. Different people have different characters, that suit (or don't suit) the roles they play.

I also see character as two mutually balancing traits, a model which neatly fits the traditional Chinese notion of *yang* and *yin*. In this tradition, every force has its opposite, and is given value by that opposite. Neither yang nor yin is 'better' than the other. They are complementary, combining to create a bigger whole. The world shifts each day between yin and yang: when you sleep at night, it is dark and cold (yin characteristics); when you wake up, you become active in the day which is warm and bright (yang). This repeated cycle provides the balance for well-being. Likewise, the human character at times needs to be strong and forceful (yang) and other times understanding and sensitive (yin). Valuing both and being able to 'be' one of these at the appropriate time is a sign of having a balanced character.

| Conductor | Vision | Character | |
|---|---|---|---|
| | | Yang | Yin |
| Leadership | Compass | Boss | Coach |
| Operations & Finance | Architect | Express train | Alarm bell |
| Sales & Marketing | Radar | Fox | Friend |

With these three concepts – vision and character (yang and its complement yin) – we have the top axis of the matrix.

## The 'Three Capability Sets'

This section covers the vertical axis of the Matrix: leadership, finance and operations and sales and marketing.

After my talk with John, I understood that a business leader has to have good ability in all areas of business. He had eight directors, however, which would make my model too cumbersome to be of practical use. After a lot of thinking, discussion and experimentation, I concluded that three essential areas of expertise were big enough to capture what the leader needs to master, yet small enough to be workable. I call these areas the 'Three Capability Sets'. These are leadership itself, plus the technical disciplines of operations and finance, and the more people-based disciplines of sales and marketing.

Practitioners of operations and finance or sales and marketing may insist that their discipline is not 'about technical skills' or 'about people', but a mixture of both. My response is to agree, but to point out that this model is not about operations, finance or sales in themselves but about the aspects of those activities that a leader needs to grasp.

In business, it is likely that a new leader will already be skilled at an area of the operations and finance set or at an area of the sales and marketing set. They will also probably be less familiar with the other set and its ways. It is a core theme of this book that to step up to leadership, a leader will need to embrace his or her weaker 'other' set, as well as pure leadership.

### A brief self-assessment exercise

In the diagram below, simply give yourself marks out of ten for your current actual strength in each area. Be realistic, both about your current strength and about what constitutes a ten. In this exercise, ten is neither Nelson Mandela in leadership nor George Soros in finance; it is a level that you regard as excellent but realistically achievable. Just mark with a pencil or pen, where you are right now (not where you would like to be.)

| | | |
|---|---|---|
| Leadership | 1_____ | 10 |
| Operations and finance | 1_____ | 10 |
| Sales and marketing | 1_____ | 10 |

When you have done this, repeat the exercise and make a mark for the level you wish to acquire and think you could acquire with a practical amount of effort (and time). By all means, aim high – but if you want ten in all three sets, consider if the amount of work you would need to put in to get to that level is truly doable. For instance, are you really willing to spend several weeks a year to keep up with social media platforms to gain a ten at sales and marketing, or would a seven or eight do? Remember that John's maxim was 'better than average'.

Sometimes people object to this: an attendee at one of my leadership courses said, 'If I can't be truly excellent at something, then there is no point in doing it all'. This type of perfectionist thinking can undermine the journey to becoming a rounded leader. (I shall say more about the common inner drive to 'be perfect' in Appendix B.)

Now you have completed the exercise, note which areas seem a stretch for you and be curious why.

I hope that this book will provide you with answers on how to progress – and how to get around inner barriers which might stop you: I have often found that it is not a lack of skill in an area, but a lack of belief in the desirability or the possibility of acquiring that skill that holds people back. (See Appendix A for more on this topic.)

Refer back to this section after you have finished reading the book and repeat the exercise – you may be surprised to find that your rating has already changed.

The Three Capability Sets give us the vertical axis of the Matrix

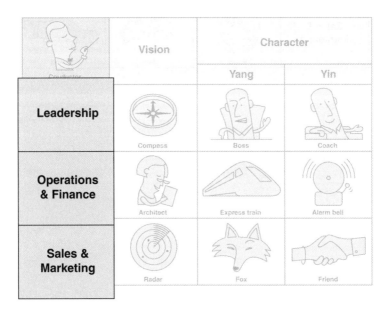

Combining these 'Three Capability Sets' with the top axis of vision and character (yin and yang) you have the Leadership Matrix Model containing the nine archetypes. I will explain the 'conductor' later in the book.

The following chapters will discuss this Matrix row by row, with one chapter for leadership, one for operations and finance and one for sales and marketing. In these chapters, I shall describe each respective archetype and its associated shadow.

| Conductor | Vision | Character | |
|---|---|---|---|
| | | **Yang** | **Yin** |
| **Leadership** | Compass | Boss | Coach |
| **Operations & Finance** | Architect | Express train | Alarm bell |
| **Sales & Marketing** | Radar | Fox | Friend |

# 2  Leadership

This is about strategy, culture, inspiration, fighting for the organisation and developing and supporting talent.

| | Vision | Character | |
|---|---|---|---|
| | | Yang | Yin |
| **Leadership** | Compass | Boss | Coach |
| Operations & Finance | Architect | Express train | Alarm bell |
| Sales & Marketing | Radar | Fox | Friend |

When I transitioned into leadership, I was very similar to the numerous coaching clients (and business contacts) that I have since worked with: although it was my own business, I was effectively an overworked manager, highly frustrated as to why I had so much to do and why the people who reported to me seemed unable to do things right. What I lacked was any real understanding of what leadership was and how little time I actually spent on it.

Leadership is a skill, just like any other business function, and needs to be valued as such. Modern managers are often so squeezed by huge work demands that they fail to grow this essential area. Part of their leadership journey will be to learn how to claw back that necessary time – otherwise, it is their superiors who will benefit from all their diligent work and they will eventually be left behind.

I recall the moment that was a last straw for me. I had a pile of papers on my desk and loads of emails; I was getting more and more aggravated as I read them, saying to myself, 'Why has no one dealt with this? Why do I have to deal with everything?' Then I had a sudden moment of realisation: 'I don't need to get this stuff done; I need to work out why I am doing it'. I called a rising star in my company and asked her to simply take all the letters on my desk and deal with them herself. Anything she needed help with, I would be there. From then on, I saw my role as giving away as much work as possible and coined the (somewhat smug) motto: 'If I am doing something, I am doing something wrong, because someone else should be doing it.'

There is a saying that a general needs to go up the side of a high hill to survey the terrain and remove him- or herself from the battlefield. With this in mind and armed with a choice of readings inspired by Stephen Covey and Hyrum Smith, I headed for a self-styled retreat in a lovely hillside hotel in Vence in the south of France. An unusual activity for me then, I spent the daytime contemplating my values, the roles I play in life and drafting various versions of a personal mission statement: what was important to me and where was I going. This structured self-reflection took me around a week. Back at home, some people laughed at the idea that I was taking time off to write my mission statement. However, I just knew something had to change. I found my time spent 'on the hill' truly invigorating and profound.

Within two years my businesses had more than doubled in size. I didn't stop working, but filled much of the space I created with more productive activity. I learnt that it takes time to lead – time and energy to make new things happen. If you don't stop doing certain old things, then you won't free up the time to do new ones. It is not enough to want to change or to envisage it, you also have to put in the time and focus to make it happen.

I shall now look at the three archetypes in this row.

## The Compass

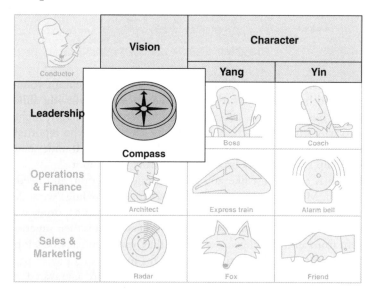

The archetype of the 'Compass' is the classic view of what leadership is about – championing a vision that others want to follow. Other thinkers use slightly different terms. Peter Senge says that a leader is a steward of a vision. Robert Dilts says that a leader needs to hold and share a vision, not possess it, as it belongs to everyone.

The Compass' main role isn't necessarily about *changing* a vision or culture (although this can be essential at times). It is about ensuring that a company stays focused and doesn't lose direction during the day-to-day grind of running its activities. For example, Apple's leadership inherited a powerful Compass from the late Steve Jobs. There was no need to change it. The need for a complete change of direction, of the kind dealt with by the Compass, is infrequent. Maybe every few years? Making such changes too often can be highly disruptive.

If change is necessary, the leader doesn't even have to be the one who creates the new vision. He or she simply has to buy into it and ensure that decisions and strategies align with it.

A personal story illustrates this well. My team and I have regular off-site team coaching sessions, with an external coach or facilitator to help work out what the business needs. During one significant session, our finance director Michael proposed a simple mission statement for the business. The moment I heard his words, I thought, 'That's it!' I was quite happy not to be the one who created it. I then had to keep the mission alive, and hold it up for everyone to see: the other directors could get lost in their 'day job' and didn't have time for this.

An inspiring vision is essential. It is the magic ingredient in great companies – creating a culture where energised and optimistic staff deliver excellent service and huge profits. It is so obvious when it is missing. However, it is not the Compass alone that delivers this. When a business is performing well, its people are aligned and all is going smoothly, the leader is best off spending his or her time on other areas of vision, which I will cover later in the chapter: the Architect (improving systems and delivery) and Radar (making changes to stay ahead of the market).

Another essential role for the Compass is to incorporate regular activities that help people stay aligned with the vision. Not only do we have these team coaching days, but also regular updates and activities with the wider staff. Initiating these is also a key role for the Compass.

The Compass is also about culture. All organisations (and departments) have a culture, whether it is deliberately created or not. However, these can be dysfunctional, and part of the job of a leader is to create one that is beneficial and lasting.

The process of creating a Compass is initiated when a leader explores these principles within themselves. That is why a leader needs to develop their own personal Compass. I shall discuss this process in greater detail in Part IV, where I will present a way of distilling values, roles and a sense of purpose into an expression of your personal vision.

An example of the importance of a personal Compass comes from a story during a seminar by Hyrum Smith. A young man was given an opportunity by his mentor, who had recently been promoted to CEO. The mentor said to the young man, 'I am going to promote you to be a director and ask you to join the board. There is only one thing I want in return – that you always vote with me'. The young man was highly conflicted by this offer. To become a director would be an amazing opportunity and his mentor had been a generous sponsor to him; he wanted to reciprocate and he valued loyalty. However, this offer clashed against another core value: integrity – to agree to this would be dishonest and he would not be able to vote according to what he considered to be the best course of action. This was a conflict of values. What was more important to him; loyalty or integrity? He chose integrity, immediately resigned, set up his own business and (according to Smith) went on to become a billionaire.

Leadership is about action based on your own core values. This is practical, as well as ethical, advice. Life is full of conflicting needs and wants – your own and those of other people – and ultimately having your own personal compass makes navigating this complex landscape much easier. Doing the right thing isn't always easy, but when you know where you are going and what is truly important to you, then you can act in a congruent way, one that is unambiguous and wholehearted. Such a basis for behaviour is essential for leaders – without it, people will not trust you. They may not always agree, but if you act within a set of core values and explain your actions, they will understand that you are at least being consistent. A personal compass involves having the self-control to coolly and consistently make major decisions based on values.

When a leader can be authentic at work, they give permission to others to be the same. A common problem in the modern workplace is that people feel they can't be themselves. This reduces their effectiveness and drains their energy. There is a commonly held misconception that people have to 'bend' themselves to fit in with the style of an organisation. I fully appreciate that each organisation has its own unique style, but a leader can harmonise with this by being both professional and real. This means appropriately expressing themselves and disclosing their feelings. It is that authentic connection with self, shared in a genuine, open yet professional way, that can really help a leader connect to, and inspire, others.

The opposite to authentic, value-driven action is reacting impulsively. Often this is done to minimise one's own fear. Fear is generally rooted in our past and possibly within our family system. It would clearly be disastrous if a leader unknowingly recreated a culture based on a dysfunctional personal history. This is where coaching or other change work comes in. A leader who is in denial of their past or is scared to 'look within' may not notice some of the issues they are causing. A leader who is truly fascinated by new ways to transcend their past and build a clear picture of the future is on their way to excellence. The needs of the business have to be put above protecting or massaging the ego of a leader. Such transformation can be painful at times, but it is far less painful than the destructive force that denial can unleash in the long run.

### Vision and personal ambition

Vision can be a very noble sounding thing – the word 'calling' was historically associated with a sense of selfless duty to do good in the world. 'Ambition', by contrast, can sound ugly and self-serving. However, business is about making money – so there is also an element of paradox in having a calling for business leadership. If you don't want to gain some of the benefits of wealth generation yourself, it is arguable that you will not be effective at generating wealth for your organisation. Good leaders do not suffer from poverty consciousness, but instead see the world as an essentially abundant place.

### 'Selling' the Compass

> 'Anything worth doing is worth doing badly, at first'.
>
> – Milton Erickson

Vision needs to be communicated in such a way that it is successfully adopted. I found when I first started discussing mission and vision with my team, their reactions were not entirely positive (see the Hippy below) – I had to vary my approach. To make this material relevant, it had to form part of wider discussions, including operational strategy. As time for communication is limited, if it is all taken up by visionary musing it will be resented. Like anything new, it takes time to get buy-in and it is well worth persevering. The Compass transformed my own business and the resulting success has made my sceptical team converts.

### The shadow

The shadow of the Compass is the Hippy.

I talked of archetypes having shadows in the introduction – the naturally occurring and potentially destructive 'mirror' of an archetype. The problems they cause can motivate positive change; alternatively, those problems can also get worse. My intention of using playful and slightly provocative terms is to form some sympathy with these traits and, hopefully, to help notice them within ourselves.

The Hippy embraces the idea of the Compass, but takes it all too far. They can alienate hard-working but naturally sceptical team members, who need a gentler, more persuasive approach. This, in turn, can upset the Hippy, who may become frustrated and condescending. In addition, the Hippy isn't aware that some of their people may have previously worked in organisations that handled the Compass so clumsily that they are already highly cynical about the subject.

As Gandhi said, 'The wise should not bewilder the ignorant'.

A leader can lose their edge if they spend too much time considering vision for their own curiosity and not focusing their energy on what the business actually needs, which is mainly the other components in the Matrix. Business is not an opportunity for a social experiment.

Coach and teacher, Jan Elfin, said, 'I try not take out the latest book I am reading on my students'. I would extend this and say don't take out your latest book on your team. The Hippy does this 'taking out' by changing the vision too frequently. The visions that emerge can also be unrealistic. A vision needs to be based on an honest understanding of how the company is now and what represents a believable shift forward.

Although businesses evolve and markets change, for the most part vision stays fixed, like a guiding star. The Hippy doesn't like the less exciting and repetitive work of doing the various activities that reignite that original vision.

The Hippy loves to teach. Although teaching is a powerful way of learning and communicating, beyond a certain point, it is better done in a different context. I started a training business partially so I could satisfy my own Hippy and stop taking it out on my staff.

### How do you acquire a Compass?

I shall look at general ways of increasing one's connection to archetypes at the end of this chapter. The material that follows is more specific to the Compass.

As I said above, a key to having a vision for your business is to have one for yourself. Set up your own personal compass by completing the exercises in the Mission and vision workbook that makes up Part IV.

Continuous learning is also part of this process. Attending courses and joining groups and clubs can be very helpful. Stephen Covey said, 'Leaders are readers'. Read widely, not just business or self-help books. Biographies, history, science and literature can nourish this archetype. Biographies don't all have to be inspirational: one can also learn a lot from people who had serious flaws, who maybe lacked some of the archetypes. I am also a great fan of audio programmes, especially Desert Island Discs, the BBC radio programme with thousands of interviews (available online at bbc.co.uk/DID).

# Business seasons

Sometimes vision does have to change. I find the metaphor of seasons helpful here. In nature there are four seasons, but in business these are effectively grouped into two phases:

*Phase 1* is 'business as usual'. This encompasses spring, summer and autumn, a time I call the 'California summer'. Spring is when new seeds are planted. It is an optimistic time, although there is a sense of anxiety: will the planting take? Summer is when vigilance is required to make sure the seedlings survive and grow. It is a hard and unrewarding period of work without much benefit, but with the hope that soon effort will be rewarded. Autumn is harvest time, when there is abundance and feasting. There is enough food to plant more right now, but it is also essential to put something away for winter.

Most healthy businesses will have various projects in spring, summer and autumn stages, with some old ones bearing fruit and some new ones just starting out. As Joe Girard said, 'The wonderful thing about business is that you can reap and sow at the same time'.

*Phase 2* is winter, when business is about survival. Unlike the real seasons, the arrival of commercial winter is fairly unpredictable. It may not happen for many years, but when it does happen, it does so quickly. It can then last a long time: a recession, changing markets, new competition, becoming a take-over target or a major disaster with lasting consequences such as a fire, litigation or the loss of a major customer – these things do not go away fast.

During winter the focus is on survival. Hopefully there was sufficient put aside during the autumn to keep the business alive. But even if there was, winter usually means radical cost-cutting, giving up on vanity projects and shrinking the business to focus on core profitable activities. As winter continues, your 'business-as-usual' friends can turn against you – suppliers can become litigious and banks restrict credit. Alan Clark said of politics, 'There are no true friends … Everyone is a shark waiting for the first sign of blood'. Fortunately, in business there is sometimes more generosity during the California summer, but during the Arctic winter Mr Clark has it right.

A sudden shift to winter requires a rapid change in culture, but the arrival of spring has its challenges, too. A winter business can become ossified by not changing or innovating for years, and miss out on new opportunities that a business in its California summer would grasp. When winter is over, a leader will have to remind everyone that this is the case. There will often be resistance to the necessary change of attitudes and practices; partly for fear that winter isn't really over, but also because people have a natural hostility to taking on the extra work that the change will require. There is a natural lag before the new work produces actual results.

Leaders can be at their most vulnerable at a change of season. Often leaders who are good at growing a business are not good at shrinking one and vice versa. A change of season often means a change of leader: to have a stable leadership career means that you need to be 'better than average' at both.

## The Boss

| | Vision | Character | |
|---|---|---|---|
| Conductor | | Yang | Yin |
| **Leadership** | Compass | **Boss** | Coach |
| Operations & Finance | Architect | Express train | Alarm bell |
| Sales & Marketing | Radar | Fox | Friend |

The energy of the Boss is in the ability to say 'no' firmly, but in a grounded way – people know when a clear and powerful 'no' has been delivered. The Boss has power; people don't want to mess with this archetype. The Boss is also a fighter, it doesn't give up easily. It is relentless – people who do mess with the Boss regret it and find it easier to comply than face the wrath of the Boss. The Boss also gives the people within an organisation a sense of protection and advocacy. You want the Boss on your side. The Boss is respected.

Archetype psychologists often talk about the Warrior archetype, and the Boss has some of these qualities. This does not make him or her violent. Quite the opposite. The qualities of a powerful Warrior are those of stillness and of courage. Stillness is the ability to quiet oneself, to silently observe what threats are in the environment, so that the Warrior is ready to fight from a place of 'relaxed readiness'. Courage is to then to fight in spite of any fear these threats may cause – it is not an absence of fear.

The Boss is proactive, 'at cause'. The leaders I have come across tended to naturally take on far wider responsibilities than their colleagues when they started in their career. 'That isn't my job' doesn't seem to be in their vocabulary. The individuals who take this responsibility tend to get noticed and become 'in demand', which increases their power and influence within the business. Eventually, major decisions are not made without their blessing and input. Many leaders I have coached didn't set out to achieve power; they acquired power more as a by-product of their attitude and commitment to the wider needs of the business. Promotion on its own doesn't make one a leader – a leader will be judged based on who they are and what they do.

The Boss, like all the archetypes, is instinctive – it can sense when someone is sincere, a time-waster or worse. Its strategy for dealing with this is direct and firm.

Here is an example of how I used Boss energy to deal with a potential business partner who turned out to be a highly negative corporate predator. He was setting up an investment fund and wanted to use our management services once he had attracted a major investor. With his impressive city background, he brought the great and the good to our offices, and we took a lot of time demonstrating our systems to these potential investors and reassuring them how safe these systems were. However, as soon as he had a deal with a leading financial institution, he changed the terms of our deal in a way that would have made us a loss, and set up his own management business instead. This was outrageous, as we had been instrumental in winning the deal for him. To add insult to injury, he then recruited one of our team.

It was time for me to use the Boss. I called him up and said, 'It would be unfortunate if people began to think you made it a habit of stabbing them in the back'. He became very aggravated and replied, 'Are you accusing me of stabbing you in the back?' In a controlled but clear and powerful voice, I replied, 'No. I said very clearly, it would be unfortunate *if* people thought that about you. Therefore, what I want is a written agreement protecting my business. Am I making myself clear?' After that conversation, I obtained a written agreement and knew he would never cross me again. He didn't.

### The shadow

In teaching this model, I have found that the Boss is often an archetype that people have a problem with. I often hear, 'I used to have a boss who was really mean to me, and I will never be like that'. However, when I ask these same people what a leader would be like who lacked Boss energy, they always reply, 'No good'.

So why is there so much controversy about this role? The answer lies in the shadow of the Boss, which is the Bully. Commonly, people will have experienced unpleasant bosses, teachers or family members in their past and dislike traits such as bullying, aggression and violence. People often confuse these negative traits with the positive ones of the Boss. This confusion can lead people to throw out the baby with the bathwater. (In reality, if people bullied you consistently in the past, they actually lacked appropriate Boss energy.)

Yet the boundary between the Boss and the Bully is not always clear. My experience is that people with strong Boss energy can flip into bullying at times. The wise leader is aware when it is necessary to be highly assertive, but also needs to become sensitive to the point at which they are crossing a line and their Boss energy is turning into Bully. At that point they pull back, ensuring they don't go too far and alienate people or destroy relationships.

People lacking sufficient Boss energy can also switch to the Bully under pressure – unable to assert their needs, they become aggressive, often in frustration that they feel they aren't being listened to.

### How do you acquire Boss energy?

If you are of a gentle disposition, you do not have to undergo a radical personality transformation to gain a sufficient Boss. Confront any negative beliefs about 'your place' and leadership (see Appendix A). Develop a sense of when Boss energy is appropriate, and then 'fake it to make it' when you know such moments have come. Watch out for when you find yourself using shadows – bullying, hiding, manipulation, whining – to deal with stress or conflict, and change your behaviour when you notice this.

Books can help you connect with your natural boss. In the long run, you will find your own sources of inspiration. I like Susan Jeffers' *Feel the Fear and Do It Anyway,* Jack Welch's *Jack: Straight from the Gut* and Marcus Aurelius' *Meditations*.

Mindfulness will also help you develop those still, Warrior qualities I mentioned above. (It has a role in developing all the archetypes. See Parts II and III.)

Cardiovascular exercise is also important way of expressing this archetype.

If you can practice a form of martial art or boxing, that can also be useful. The soft martial art of Tai Chi is a gentle and mindful way of expressing Warrior energy.

## The Coach

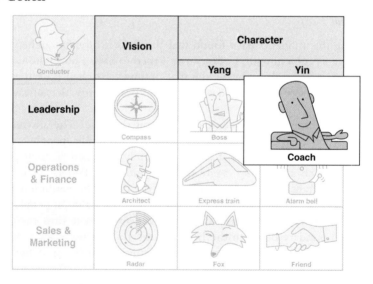

The Coach is the yin energy to balance that of the Boss. It has a sense of compassion and genuine caring for others. The Boss may engender respect, but the Coach attracts genuine loyalty.

My formal coach training started rather spontaneously after a recommendation. I started a two-day coaching programme and signed up without even knowing what coaching was. On the course, I was assigned to work with a young woman who was a newly qualified and enthusiastic coach. She told me about a problem she was having. I listened, then proceeded to give her the benefit of my years of 'wisdom' in business. To my absolute shock, she lost her temper and started scolding me, 'I want you to coach me. This is my time and I want to be listened to – I don't want to hear your advice!!!'

I realised that I was completely out of my depth with this 'coaching stuff'. I had spent all my life not really listening, but filtering out anything that wasn't of interest to me. If I did listen, it was usually with an intention of persuading someone to see things my way. I had never learnt how to simply listen.

Coaching is about learning how to listen and to allow other people to fully express their feelings without agreeing or disagreeing, just providing a safe space for them to feel heard. It is the ability to be with somebody and not use the time while they talk to think about what to say in return ourselves. It is attending to someone else with genuine curiosity and empathy, 'fascinated by another expressing themselves'. It is an appropriately humbling experience to share a sense that you are both human beings. This is *mindful listening*.

This may all sound a bit touchy-feely, but I have found the ability to listen in this way is excellent in building loyalty and trust with people. When they feel understood, I sense a new bond and level of trust has emerged.

Coaches also deliberately look at the other person and carefully watch out for subtle clues. These might include facial expressions (such as frowning or pursed lips), fidgeting and gesturing, little barely audible sighs, rigid posture, eyes looking down. This skill can easily be transferred to business, where learning to listen and look with this level of attentiveness can help you find when someone is sincere about something or to spot people who may be withholding something important. It is the so-called intuition that is so often spoken about. Coach and neuro linguistic programming (NLP) training teach you to do this deliberately. I found that after a time it slipped into my repertoire of skills, and now I don't know how I could have managed without it (especially in complex, high-stakes negotiations).

The Coach has a belief that people need more than anything to feel understood and their opinion valued (even if you do not necessarily agree with them). This is essential to attracting and retaining talented people, which is arguably the most important quality for a leader.

A key member of staff handed in their resignation during a particularly challenging time just after the 2008 economic crisis. I sensed he was very angry and I let him express himself fully. I then looked him in the eye and said, 'I really understand what you have said and I really get that you are angry and frustrated. I ask you to trust me for two more weeks and see if I can do something different. If by then you are still unhappy you can leave, but please give me a little more time'.

He stayed on and still works with me at a very senior level today. We have both benefitted enormously from our continued collaboration.

The Coach is able to convey genuine interest for people, not in a sentimental way, but in a professional way, where he or she is able to spend that little extra time to listen and talk. This type of engagement helps a leader build their 'tribe', who may even follow them into different organisations.

Soon after I met my wife Anna, I spent some time with her and one of her direct reports. It was interesting to witness the mix of active listening and coaching that she naturally gave. I understood then why she had risen quickly and managed teams across the world for one of Britain's largest banks. She offered both support and guidance and I noticed how she listened intently as the person really opened up to her and started sharing his concerns. A few months later, Anna changed her role and I went to her leaving party. Many of her staff seemed genuinely saddened by her departure. As the years have passed, she regularly hears from old colleagues who are keeping an 'iron in the fire' in case an opening to work with her again comes up in the future.

Coaching involves techniques for asking people questions that will help them work out how to achieve certain goals. This is part of the difference between a manager's and a leader's approach to working with their team. Competent direct reports prefer to be asked how they intend to achieve something and thereafter you can make any comments or suggestions. They are more likely to be committed to a course of action they have constructed themselves.

The Coach has a passion for developing talent within the organisation. In the business classic, *In Search of Excellence*, Tom Peters says that the greatest pride of many of America's top CEOs, looking back upon their careers, was not the big deals but the handful of people they spotted and mentored who had now risen high in their own careers. Often the leader's greatest legacy is not the material achievements, but the people they have touched and helped on their way. Known for his relentless approach to talent management, Jack Welch of General Electric flew around the world and challenged all the company's numerous business leaders to prove they continually improved staff.

Here are some wider benefits of the Coach:

1  Self-Coaching. Leaders are able to coach themselves, ensuring they can remain self-aware and self-critical – especially in a crisis.
2  Charisma. Mindfulness is at the heart of the Coach. When a leader is fully present with people, they sense that presence and often use that word. 'The CEO has a real presence'. It is part of charisma. Mindfulness and genuine listening are key ingredients to becoming a great leader.

3  Wider stakeholder relationships. Coach energy is also useful in sales, customer relations, managing upward or even purchasing roles – the same type of presence and genuine interest creates excellent relationships with customers and suppliers.

I have been surprised by just how many top executives are very well versed in all kinds of psychological, and even esoteric, studies as well as the old nuts and bolts approach to managing people. The traditional command and control ways may have worked a decade ago – but the new breed of leaders understands the need for coaching approaches. I have come across many, who have become significantly competent coaches themselves and are excellent at retaining and growing talent within their teams.

However, there are potential conflicts. One of the key components of being a professional coach is a *lack of agenda*. I also work as a professional coach. My coaching clients' decisions do not impact me – therefore I don't need to steer them in any particular direction. My job is to help them have a conversation with themselves and to hold up a metaphorical mirror so they can clearly see their own issues and make decisions accordingly.

As a leader, of course, I do have an agenda for my staff.

It is therefore essential that leaders create clear boundaries and avoid the confusion that their empathetic Coach can create. If someone reveals something about themselves that represents a threat to the organisation, necessary action will be taken against them. If this threat is revealed during a perceived confidential 'coaching session', that individual will feel manipulated. When news of this gets out, this can severely undermine the reputation of a leader. This neatly leads onto the shadow.

### The shadow

The shadow of the Coach is the Psychoanalyst, who oversteps boundaries and cannot detect when the Coach is unwelcome or inappropriate.

I have had various experiences in my career as a trainer of coaching, of well-meaning students returning to their office environment and misusing their new skills on unhappy staff. For someone to have an intimate psychological relationship with an individual who has power over them is highly problematic. Conversely, such a relationship also can be used by cunning staff as a way of gaining influence (by connecting to a leader's Psychoanalyst).

### How do you develop your Coach archetype?

If you are a direct person and like to speak your mind, you may find all of this a bit soft and irritating. But, as with the Boss above, you do not have to undergo a radical personality transformation to gain a sufficient Coach. Hopefully this chapter has convinced you of the benefits, but test it for yourself. Develop a sense when Coach energy is appropriate, 'fake it to make it' when you know such moments have come, and see if it works. You might be surprised – I was!

I highly suggest you learn the fundamentals of coaching. There are a number of good courses around – I run them at NLP School (www.nlpschool. com), which ranges much wider than pure NLP. There are many others, too.

Another way of learning coaching skills is to receive coaching yourself. I found it fascinating to watch a person listen to me so attentively and then suddenly ask me a 'killer question' – how did they do this?

Certain classic texts can also teach you a lot about coaching.

- My own *How to Coach with NLP*
- *The Seven Habits of Highly Effective People* by Steven Covey
- *Co-Active Coaching* by Laura Whitworth, Karen Kimsey-House, Henry Kimsey-House and Phillip Sandahl
- *Coaching for Performance* by John Whitmore
- *Coach to Awakener* by Robert Dilts
- *The Inner Game of Tennis* by Timothy Gallwey (the book that started off the modern coaching movement)

## Balancing the leadership archetypes

Now we have discussed the Compass, Boss and Coach, along with their respective shadows, the Hippy, Bully and Psychoanalyst, I would like to discuss briefly how these qualities interact.

If someone lacks Boss energy, but is strong on Coach and Compass, they will tend to lack power. Even with a big vision, it will be hard to attract people to work with them, as they do not offer the sense of protection that goes with Boss energy. People want someone tough in their corner at certain times and, regardless how psychologically savvy and visionary that person is, without sufficient Boss energy a leader will not be trusted to stand up when the going gets difficult.

If someone lacks Coach energy, but is strong on Boss and Compass, you have a powerful and tough visionary, but without the ability to value people appropriately. They don't build a loyal team and can become an Atlas figure, with all the crushing weight on their shoulders as they strive for greatness. They can also create enemies.

If someone lacks Compass, but is strong on Boss and Coach, you have a stressed manager; someone who will work harder and harder, spiralling down into being overwhelmed as the workload grows and the motivation of their team diminishes.

## The art of acquiring archetypes

One of the first jobs of a leader is to lead themselves into acquiring the skills they will need in their 'designed future'. It is hard to be prescriptive about this area – but here are some general tips.

### Know what you don't know

A great skill is to understand what you don't know. Spot the gaps in your knowledge and do all that you can to fill them.

### Talk to experts

John, the entrepreneur whose comments first set me on the road to this model, said, 'When I started my business I found an accountant in the yellow pages – she taught me double entry book keeping in about ten minutes and that was really all I needed for the first five years of my business'.

If there's a large area which is new to you, get an overview of it. When I realised how little I knew about human resources (HR), I asked an HR director to talk about her job. She gave me a breakdown of all the key functions in HR and I came away with a nice clear understanding that I could later 'drill down' into. You need this for each core function in business: what do they do and how do they do it?

### Be curious

At certain points in your life, it is good to become passionate about gaining a certain skill in greater depth. After going on a time management course, I became almost obsessed with the subject for a while, reading widely and building my own task management systems. Then another gap in my knowledge became apparent, and I made myself head off in pursuit of filling that. Years later, I realised my time management skills had dated and revisited the subject (David Allen's ideas on email management were particularly helpful).

Leaders need a passion to understand how a business works and what makes people tick. Be a Renaissance person; enjoy gaining a wide range of new passions and skills. Be endlessly curious. Such an approach to learning stands you in good stead for future leadership challenges in a fast-changing world.

### Find role models and copy them

I recall a discussion with two seasoned directors of an insurance company. Reflecting on their careers, they both said they had copied various people who they found impressive. They didn't 'become' these people, but noticed how they behaved in various situations and tried to emulate them. This is how young children learn – fully absorbed by the activities of the 'amazingly competent' grownups that surround them and wanting to copy them. The idea that this sort of learning stops when we mature is wrong and unhelpful. One of the key questions people ask me is 'How am I meant to acquire all of these archetypes?' The answer is find some people who have them and copy them.

Rather than seeking to copy someone in general, look to gain a specific skill from them. Find an *exemplar* (a person you want to copy), spend some time with them in a relevant work situation and watch what they do. Afterwards, talk to them about it.

I went on a sales visit with a top sales person. The first thing I noticed was that he didn't even do the pitching, but let another team member do it, while he looked intently round at the customer team. After the meeting, I asked him what he was doing during the quiet time when the pitch was being delivered. His reply was, 'Obviously I was looking for signs of who was deferring to whom. I noticed who made eye contact and watched little nods and expressions. That's how I worked out who the decision maker was and who was also necessary for that decision. The person who invited us in wasn't one of the people needed for the decision'.

You are looking for 'the difference that makes the difference', but it is hard to predict what this will be. You won't discover anything new, if you don't experience these situations with an open mind and spirit of genuine curiosity.

NLP has a formal methodology for this process called 'modelling'.

### Learn from mistakes

Another way I learnt was to watch people doing things 'wrong' – effectively modelling *not* doing what they did. Be curious as to what are the critical flaws that could undermine success. When I was young, I had a charismatic and dynamic boss who didn't handle stress well – he become extremely aggressive at times, alienating and destroying relationships that took him ages to build up. This anger was the shadow side of his passion for his business. I also feel passionate about my business and get very upset when I feel badly let down; but this lesson from my youth stuck. I have learnt to control my temper and avoid breaking relationships, although at times I have come close. I know how far to go, by remembering what 'too far' looked like.

# 3 Operations and finance

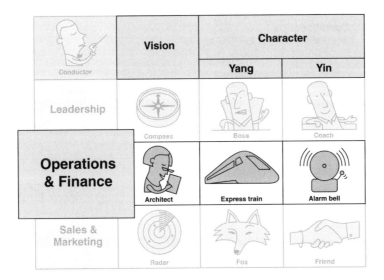

This is the business of making things, getting things done, managing resources, and developing an acute awareness of impending crises.

This chapter focuses on tasks and resources within a business. For individual specialists, often these roles are separate: the Chief Operations Officer (COO) and the Chief Financial Officer (CFO). However, I have grouped these roles together, partially for simplicity, but also because they *are* sometimes combined, typically when an accountant starts to broaden their focus to the operational and legal aspects of the business. This is the role of what was in the past called the commercial director – someone responsible for the legal, financial, infrastructure and delivery aspects of a business and who had to find a balance between the competing demands of these functions.

Typically, the COO would like unlimited resources to invest in new technologies, delight the customer and reward the staff. Often the CFO underinvests in these things, but ensures that money doesn't run out. This is another example of creative tension; it is essential for a well-run organisation to do a good enough job with limited resources.

## The Architect

I call the quality of vision in operations and finance the Architect.

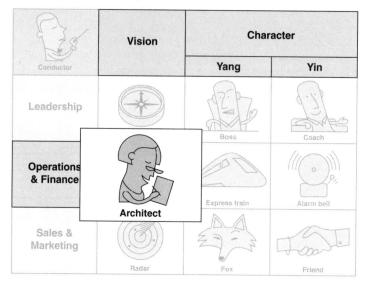

> 'Everything should be made as simple as possible, but not any simpler'
> – Albert Einstein.

The Architect has a passion for designing systems that deliver consistent results easily. Linked to this is a clear understanding of investment and of creating processes that are both cost effective and help a business grow.

This is the visionary work that a leader does on a more regular basis. While the Compass is required from time to time for an overall guiding vision, the Architect implements that vision in a practical, outcome-orientated way.

In many ways, the Architect is the distinguishing factor between a manager and a leader – a manager executes the processes of their superiors while a leader looks to evolve and replace processes. This involves a wider understanding of the way competitors are operating and a willingness to question established procedures that have become redundant. The online world has made this all the more important – a leader needs to protect their business unit from competition by rivals with more elegant online processes.

McDonald's is an example of a traditional business that is built on Architecture: rigorous training and implementation of standardised processes across the world. An employee of McDonald's shared with me that they had a large manual to cover how to clean the chip fryer, which had to be done daily. Franchisees who had invested heavily into running an outlet would be removed if standards were not maintained.

A personal example was taking time out to develop a suite of standard letters to speed up responses to the vast quantities of similar questions I received from solicitors when a property changed hands. Not only did it save time when I began managing a larger portfolio, it later enabled my unqualified employees to deal competently with solicitors.

Although this may be obvious, a leader needs to truly value good processes and be prepared to put in the time and investment upfront to build and evolve systems to cope with future needs. You envision an elegant delivery culture.

The Architect is a favourite archetype of mine. I see business as the art of building sustainable processes. A great restaurant offers not just good but consistently good food. If the recipe changed for a dish I liked each time I went, I wouldn't go back – I want the fish or the soup or the noodles at my favourite food outlets to taste the same each time. So it is with most aspects of business: the need to build an efficient machine. As John Zeale, an early insurance supplier, told me, 'Business is like building a sausage machine, but instead of sausages it outputs money'. He went on to say, 'Then you need to find someone else to turn the handle'.

The world's greatest businesses have great and reliable processes. I recall an interview with the CEO of Toyota where he responded to a criticism that the Japanese just produce copies of things made in the west and lacked creativity. He countered this brilliantly by saying that all businesses copy each other, but the Japanese had been highly creative in their production processes, and that was their secret for producing superior cars.

The Architect also needs to ensure that processes don't become so numerous and cumbersome that people have to get around them to do their jobs. Sometimes processes have to be removed. Peter Drucker observed, 'Nothing is more useless than doing efficiently that which doesn't need to be done at all'.

It isn't practical for the Architect to intimately understand every process. Indeed, some organisations are so vast that they have more processes than any individual can actually learn.

However, ensuring that a culture of refining and implementing processes exists is at the heart of the job of the Architect – especially to avoid catastrophes. There needs to be a set of back-up processes for emergencies: is there an emergency number or standard email to warn of dangerous events? After BP's acquisition of Amoco, it became one of the world's largest oil companies. It had huge numbers of processes for production and safety. But the Deepwater Horizon spillage in the Gulf of Mexico still happened. Tony Hayward, the CEO, lost his job, and the company is estimated to have lost over $60 billion from the disaster. There are conflicting reports of who exactly was to blame – but it does seem that a drive to keep the oil wells open may have overridden established safety protocols. It is a salutary lesson; a leader needs to instil a culture with the correct balance between rigorous processes and profitability.

This is the type of leadership work of the Architect – to create an efficient culture that can easily access the right processes, along with instilling an Alarm Bell (see below) to avoid catastrophes.

The Architect also understands the financial structure of the business. It develops a felt sense of how money flows around the system. It develops a gut instinct for when things are getting tight or where cash is haemorrhaging out.

The Architect keeps a clear head when assessing risk. He or she goes into any decision armed with the knowledge that the consequences of that decision will be closely monitored, and that if it begins to go wrong, action will be taken. The Architect is essentially an optimist, and trusts that money wisely spent will yield a growing return.

### The shadow

'If it ain't broke – don't fix it.'
— Bert Lance (1970s businessman and advisor to President Jimmy Carter)

The shadow of the Architect is the Tinkerer.

The Tinkerer keeps changing their design, becomes inefficient and, in some cases, becomes completely unable to implement anything new, as everything gets stuck in that early phase. This can be driven by an unrealistic desire for perfection, but there is also something fun in playing with toys and not actually having to face the reality of putting things out there. Indecisiveness can also play into fear of making the wrong decision – it can feel better to stay at the drawing board than risk actually completing something.

The Tinkerer loves designing and implementing new systems and software programmes, even if there is no real need to do so. This reminds me of the Charlie Chaplin film *Modern Times*, when a Tinkerer has built a machine to automate the consumption of soup including a robot spoon and napkin. It goes horribly wrong. The manual version of the spoon and the napkin still works best.

The Tinkerer likes nothing more than new technology. The Architect needs to embody the role of Chief Information Office (CIO) – providing a balance between the need for periodic updating of systems and the unnecessary implementation of new technologies. The motto 'All that glitters is not gold' is needed here.

### How do you acquire the Architect?

Get to understand in some significant detail how each department in your organisation functions. If you are not from one of these disciplines, spend time with operations specialists and accountants to understand their mindsets.

Develop an instinct for processes. The Architect has a natural feel for whether processes are effective and usable, or rigid and actually have lots of 'get arounds'. On visits to departments, get a feel for whether people are overwhelmed by poorly implemented new technologies or systems.

Master a business sector. The Architect likes to stay in the same sector for most of their career. Although people can change sectors, I would advise against doing this too often. I have found that leaders who frequently move from fashion, to banking, to manufacturing, to media (and so on) can lack connection to what the business actually does on a day-to-day basis.

## The Express Train

For many, the Express Train alone is what leadership is all about: someone who makes it happen. Often organisations become so bureaucratic that there is a great sense of frustration, and people cry out for a leader who can create momentum.

Despite this, the Express Train often gets criticised as simplistic. In response to saying, 'Let's just get on with it', aspiring leaders are told that more tests need to be carried out, that more committees must consider the matter, that buy-in is needed from other stakeholders (and so on). But leaders need to have a passion for results, for action.

Sadly, this passion is often sucked out of people, who begin their careers in large organisations full of it, but slowly get ground down, at first just accepting the endless round of committees as a fact of life, then coming to believe that these things are necessary and actually a sign of 'doing it right'.

When you meet a leader, you often get a sense of someone who 'drives through' things, who won't passively accept that they can't do anything. They have an urgency to make things happen. It can manifest itself in impatience (turning into the Express Train's shadow, of which there is more below), and so, like all the archetypes, needs to be used appropriately.

What the critics of the Express Train miss is that action itself creates a whole set of new tasks and thereby new perspectives. It's only once something has begun that you can really see the consequences and form a clear, practical view of what needs to be done next. This creates an upward spiral of experimentation and dynamism. It creates a focus on outcomes. Endless 'should we/shouldn't we?' discussions get replaced by a determination to give something a small try and to see what happens.

A great motto for the Express Train is 'What's the next step?' This creates mental focus, which can otherwise be dissipated by general talk.

The Express Train is sometimes seen as something that needs to be wheeled on once a decision has been made, but it is deeper and more strategic than that. It needs to be there from the outset. It's a way of looking at the world. At its deepest level, it is about having the courage to initiate things. Action can be quite scary, but the leader dares to overcome this.

Looking back, my greatest successes in business have been a direct result of trying things that initially failed. It was the learning I got from the 'failure' that taught me how to do it right. This is a classic Express Train.

In his book *The Lean Startup*, author Eric Ries speaks of the company that created Second Life, a graphic way of using avatars for people to communicate to each other online. The founders believed that this technology would be perfect for people using social media, so they built a complex interface to various social media platforms. For example, if two Facebook friends had this program, they could communicate with each other using these avatars. The founders spent much of their budget on this. However, when they launched the program, no one used this feature. They invited a few young people to try out the program and interviewed them afterwards. It wasn't until one of them admitted that they loved the program, but wanted to use it anonymously, that they understood what was going wrong. The Express Train wouldn't waste time and money trying to anticipate everything – 'get something out there fast and find out if anyone wants it'.

### The shadow

The shadow of the Express Train is the 'Steamroller'. This is often motivated by a compulsive work ethic.

Young managers can often develop a Steamroller mentality, which works at a junior level but can be disastrous as they become more senior. They start as an effective worker and are given a small team, which they keep under tight control. Their assistants carry out orders without thinking too much. This type of small operation can yield good results with basic tasks, and the manager can get promoted as someone who gets things done. However, if their role grows to one where they have authority over more senior, experienced people, this approach will fail.

Stuck in a vicious circle, this kind of manager thinks that by becoming an increasingly aggressive Steamroller, they will somehow pressurise themselves and their team into winning results. Instead, the pressure just builds, on themselves and their team. They begin to alienate the team and the senior management that promoted them in the first place. At this point, the manager often 'moves on' and starts a new job, with a similar repeated rise and crash trajectory.

The Steamroller also makes poor decisions, sometimes impulsively, to win business, without sufficiently checking the figures. I have seen many businesses (of all sizes) taking on projects that were loss-making simply because they didn't assess them properly first. Another aspect to this can be the desire for the prestige of a big customer (see the Creep below).

### How do you acquire the Express Train?

Read *The Lean Startup*. Ries talks about new product launches and coined the term 'minimum viable product' (MVP).

Launch something basic, not with the intention of making money, but simply with the intention to learn. Don't spend too much time debating it – just get on with it (cheaply). Allow the Architect (and the Alarm Bell that follows) to stop the project if it is not viable.

Use the 'as if' frame. This brilliant idea from Robert Dilts asks you to think *as if* you have already achieved a goal, or at least *as if* you have already decided to pursue it. Pretend to go ahead with project and find out what new information you get when you take the first few (free and imagined) steps.

Read *Getting Things Done* by David Allen and *Execution* by Larry Bossidy and Ram Charan.

## The Alarm Bell

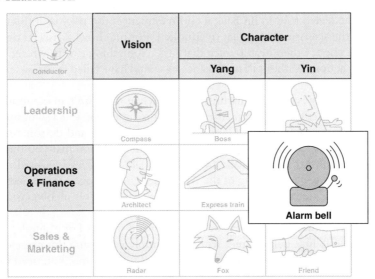

In its fullest sense, the Alarm Bell is a call to action, a deep sense that something major has changed and the organisation is suddenly in real danger.

Here is a personal story from 2008, before the start of the credit crunch. I had a general sense at the time that something bad was looming, but I remember attending a presentation where I suddenly became acutely aware that I was the only one who was seriously worried. My team were relatively young and simply didn't believe that recessions existed. I felt that their 'business as usual' attitude needed to be challenged, and asked to look at the detail behind the cashflows and sales forecasts. The figures I was shown included numbers that now looked to me excessively optimistic. I asked to see the forecast again with one large sale removed. Suddenly the graph changed shape dramatically and showed that the company would run into dire straits in a few weeks' time.

I had a strong visceral response to this – my Alarm Bell was ringing loud and clear.

My immediate reaction was still to do nothing. That is the best response to the Alarm Bell. Outwardly, stay calm and focused, while retaining your new-found sense of urgency. I went away and reflected on what to do next. The Alarm Bell had done its job: time for other energies to come to the fore. I will continue this story in Chapter 5 when discussing the Conductor below.

A gentler example of the Alarm Bell is the way I interact with my solicitor, someone for whom I have immense respect and whom I trust implicitly. He often warns me of the potential pitfalls of a course of action. When I tell him that I want to proceed anyway, he usually chuckles and accepts my decision. If, instead, he becomes agitated and continues to warn me against it, I take that as a ring from *his* Alarm Bell. I take a step back and make the effort to gain a deeper understanding of the issue at hand.

The Alarm Bell can have a physical manifestation. Investor George Soros says that he feels a pain in his back if an investment is too risky or if there is an aspect of the scenario that he has overlooked. For me, I feel a visceral tightening in my chest. I then hear a voice that says, 'Something is very wrong.' This is a call to action. Without it, my businesses would have failed at various pivotal moments.

The difficulty is that the Alarm Bell rings when there isn't an obvious solution (that is exactly why it is an Alarm Bell). It is a warning, not a solution. The next phase is to move to the Conductor (see Chapter 5) and do some testing of various courses of action. Don't jump at the first solution that you think of.

A leader needs to notice little rings of the bell, too. It can be hard to differentiate between a light ring of the Alarm Bell (when you sense something is wrong) and the fact that you are just a bit stressed out. This involves a degree of self-reflection.

A light ring can often be sorted out quickly and simply. For example, if you sense someone isn't being direct with you, simply expressing this can clear up the issue quickly. The Alarm Bell has 'guess and test' features; you need to test the situation to determine if it is a simple issue or part of a potentially much bigger problem. As well as a sign that disaster is about to strike, the Alarm Bell can also be a warning that you are *slowly* moving onto thin ice – immediate attention can avert a problem from becoming a disaster.

All this creates stress. As a leader, you will need to get used to a degree of perpetual pressure. The buck stops with you. I recall a man meeting me at a wedding before I had learnt about leadership and was effectively a stressed-out manager. He asked what I did, but before I could answer he said, 'You're a boss, aren't you?' Slightly puzzled by his assertion, I asked why he had said that. He said, 'You look like you have the weight of the world on your shoulders. Do you?' I was a bit stunned, but reflecting later I had to admit that I did.

Learning to manage your stress is an essential leadership skill – mindfulness is a powerful tool for this.

### The shadow

The shadow of the Alarm Bell is the Headless Chicken. Although a slightly gruesome metaphor, it is painfully apt. Chickens will frequently run around for a couple of minutes after they have been beheaded.

Business presents the leader with frequent challenges and numerous decisions. The leader needs to stay cool even when others around are panicking. Once the leader is unnerved, by either an overly aggressive or fearful response, the entire organisation can become flustered.

The Headless Chicken is also likely to emerge when a leader has taken on too much. Often small issues magnify under stress and it can be hard to differentiate between a true Alarm Bell and an alarmist article read in a newspaper. If you find yourself becoming very emotionally overwhelmed on a regular basis, I would suggest coaching, mindfulness and other stress management approaches. A leader needs to manage their energy and frequent Headless Chicken events will make them 'run on empty'. A leader needs energy in reserve to deal with a true crisis.

### How do you acquire the Alarm Bell?

Mindfulness, a physical practice such as yoga or Tai Chi or a professional deep tissue massage will help you become aware of where you hold tension in yourself. Most people hold tension in specific parts of their body, which should make pain in that area a perfect Alarm Bell, like George Soros' backache. However, we can become so used to this discomfort that we stop noticing it. Start noticing it again. Where do you 'tighten up' at times of stress?

Another way is to recall memories of when you 'knew' something was wrong. Become aware of any tension in your body at this time, but also notice any internal images or self-talk. I suggest you follow one of the mindfulness processes in Part III and then focus on a specific memory when your Alarm Bell rang. You can then benchmark your Alarm Bell for future use.

## Balancing the archetypes

With a good balance of Architect, Express Train and Alarm Bell, a business will function well, both operationally and financially.

When the Architect is lacking, a business will operate by the seat of its pants, not putting in place proper systems. This will cause unnecessary work and poor work practices. As the business grows, these 'reinventing the wheel' approaches become unsustainable. Failure by overtrading is a common fate for such businesses: a strong sales force, which is not matched by a back office capable of delivering the product or service in a timely and cost-effective manner, will be unable to meet their orders. Finances will spin out of control, with the company running out of money.

Less dramatically, poorly organised businesses can bump along, but eventually competition will make such a business unviable.

When the Express Train is lacking, you get an ossified business, where people love the existing products or services and live by the motto 'If only the world would stay the same'.

When the Alarm Bell is lacking, an incoming missile will simply not be noticed until it is too late. Businesses as large as Lehman Brothers and RBS didn't spot that large amounts of foolish decisions had been made. A deafening Alarm Bell should have rung in their leaders' ears at various points.

## Stepping up from operations and finance to leadership

The technical specialists, such as accountants, engineers and lawyers, whom I have coached and who have then become leaders, share unique issues in their leadership journey.

The main one is trust: the training and mindsets in these professions are highly risk-averse. New leaders can become over-controlling and fail to delegate sufficiently. If you fall into this trap, not only will you become a bottleneck in your organisation, you will also fail to attract and retain top quality people, who usually don't appreciate being held on a tight leash.

Accountancy is excellent training for business. However, it can be a fairly solitary profession, office-based with long periods of working with books and auditing as part of the training process. People from this background can find it hard to engage externally – with customers, salespeople and other stakeholders – and instead spend too much time in the office focusing within their mental comfort zone. Knowing when to leave your comfort zone is a challenge for all specialists who become leaders: I talk more about this later in Chapter 5 when discussing the Conductor archetype.

# Leadership and experts

An essential role of a leader is to take expert advice for the numerous 'high impact' situations that regularly occur in business. This includes external providers of expertise – lawyers, auditors, technology specialists – and those within your own organisation. Here are a few tips.

## *Challenge internal experts*

I recall a situation when my finance director said that our bank required us to make a very costly change. From my own limited knowledge, I sensed that this might be true, but that the bank could also be wrong. I insisted on seeing a top law firm. My finance director was confident about the bank's position and was slightly put out by my challenge, but he fortunately values the truth. I stuck to my guns and said, 'Indulge me, I might be right'. The lawyers confirmed my suspicion: what the bank had said was simply wrong.

## *Listen to experts but don't defer to them*

It is essential for leaders to take advice. Both internal and external experts are there to inform the leader of the consequences of different causes of action. However, it is for the leader to then decide what instructions to actually give in the light of this information. It is my firm view that no issue is 'beyond me' – I simply need to have it explained and I can then work it out.

## *Experts themselves are also perpetually learning*

The best people learn quickly and are humble about what they don't know. I have seen experts having to learn entirely new approaches, as their businesses opened to new opportunities and products. However, this can also lead some experts to be ashamed of gaps in their knowledge, which they then try and hide; make sure your internal experts consult outside ones (and let you know what they have learnt). In reality, nobody can be a master of an entire field like finance, law or technology – they are just too big. A leader needs breadth, so he or she can spot when internal experts have gaps and then ensure those gaps are filled.

## *Encourage creative tension*

My finance director and I, together, have won some great finance deals and negotiated our way out of some pretty hairy times during the credit crunch. Yes, there is tension between us, but it is creative. The Beatles often had arguments; it was their different perspectives that made the difference. Chris West helped me edit this book, and we have had many discussions – if something doesn't make sense to him, then I need to rewrite it to explain it better. If a leader works synergistically with the expert, a 'third way' will emerge, which was better than what either could think of individually. Sometimes that involves a few iterations, but it is well worth it.

# 4    Sales and marketing

| Conductor | Vision | Character | |
|---|---|---|---|
| | | Yang | Yin |
| Leadership | Compass | Boss | Coach |
| Operations & Finance | Architect | Express train | Alarm bell |
| **Sales & Marketing** | Radar | Fox | Friend |

This is about knowing the market, 'street smarts', building lasting and excellent relationships.

My first proper job was in the sales department of NCR, the American business machine company that invented the cash register. I initially applied for a job in accounts, but the person interviewing me believed I had what it took to do well in sales. I then had a second interview with a sales manager, who was concerned that my degree in maths for business was too technical. As he put it, 'Sales is not a science, it is the art of understanding and influencing people'. But I got the job, and the training and experience was probably more useful than my degree.

However, a career in sales (especially outside the United States) is often seen as low prestige; it is not widely considered a desirable profession compared to medicine, law or engineering. This is probably due to certain disreputable types of sales and marketing people: the 'Snake Oil Seller' and the practitioner of high pressure sales. Personally, I believe that there is no point trying to sell something to someone who doesn't either want it or need it: the process of selling is to make the process of buying easy for the customer. Great sales people build lasting relationships and maintain them with good service and genuine care for their customers. Leaders need to do this too. All successful leaders are good dealmakers, even if they work in the public sector: they still need to agree good terms for their organisation.

Marketing has a strong technical aspect – marketers are good data analysts – but good marketers are also excellent psychologists. They have an instinct for what customers want, and for the best ways of getting messages across to those people. They are also observers of patterns of behaviour in large groups, like academics in economics, political science or sociology; they develop a strong sense of how groups of people respond and behave.

A business leader needs a solid grasp of marketing – or at least of markets and how they change. Very few businesses survive if they don't adapt to changing customer preferences (especially in the digital world).

## Radar

| | **Vision** | **Character** | |
| --- | --- | --- | --- |
| Conductor | | **Yang** | **Yin** |
| Leadership | Compass | Boss | Coach |
| Operations & Finance | | Express train | Alarm bell |
| **Sales & Marketing** | **Radar** | Fox | Friend |

Radar is the Vision archetype for this Capability Set. It is a fascination for what is going on 'out there', both in the world generally – politically, economically, socially, technologically – and in the business's immediate environment. It is the intuition a leader develops for the market – and world – that they operate in. Surveys and data may be useful, but a leader has to interpret these with a highly critical eye. Daniel Kahneman's book *Thinking, Fast and Slow* clearly demonstrates how the choice of questions and small sample sizes can paint a wholly inaccurate picture of a market. If the Architect needs to sense when the numbers feel wrong, Radar needs to sense when patterns in the data don't feel right.

For most business leaders, inventing entirely new ranges of products may be unnecessary – though creativity remains key. Producing new products or services within an existing range (and updating old ones) still requires a fine sense of the market.

Radar also looks out for the herd mentality: if everyone believes something, it is instinctively sceptical. Not automatically contrarian, but curious. What is everyone doing? Are there opportunities to prosper by doing something different?

The market you operate in will at some point change, sometimes with unexpected radicalism. But at other times, changes get talked up beyond their significance. It can be very hard to know the difference between an over-reaction and a need for genuine change, so let's look at the shadow of Radar, the Guru.

### The shadow

The Guru operates under the deluded belief that they can see accurately into the future. They have some mystical power and get confused between a good hunch and a crystal ball.

The saying 'nothing fails like success' really comes to life with the Guru. It is very hard to be absolutely certain about your feelings in a market – even George Soros, who made £1bn from Black Wednesday in 1992, lost $600m on the Japanese yen soon afterwards. Even after a run of successful predictions, there is always a need for both humility and testing.

If you sense that something needs to change radically or an amazing opportunity might be missed, the question then arises: can you pursue this without 'betting the business'?

A number of highly successful entrepreneurs do bet their businesses and win. Rupert Murdoch has done this a number of times, as did Steve Jobs. But most leaders don't. A leader's main job is to be creative enough to keep the business moving up and cautious enough to prevent business failure, risking everyone else's jobs and all the shareholders' funds.

My Uncle Milton made the mistake of believing his own Guru. He reckoned that profit margins with large retailers in his clothing business were shrinking. He took his eyes off the ball in dealing with this sector, and went on record calling their buyers highly offensive names. Within a week of the publication of these comments, most of his customers had left and cancelled their orders. He switched markets to niche retailers, as his Guru told him to, but in a way that had cut off his traditional source of business in a totally unnecessary fashion.

I worked for him one summer in my late teens, and it proved very instructive. I was impressed by his drive and creativity, but the best lesson I learnt was about his tendency to undermine his success by a deluded belief in his own genius. When I went into business myself, I was determined to maintain humility and humanity, and not to believe my own bullshit. I would, I felt, then have a chance for lasting success. I am still grateful to him for that lesson.

I should also point out that Guru behaviour isn't always backing wild new projects. Downsizing during a boom period is also the mark of a Guru: moving to winter mode when it is actually still the middle of summer, and missing the harvest.

The line between Radar and Guru can be very fine and hard to delineate. It is also subjective and easy to view with the benefit of hindsight. The maxim 'don't bet the business' can help if you are unsure which side of the line you are on.

Having ways of staying grounded also helps me not drift into Guru. My training business puts me in front of people on a regular basis who don't know me and who will judge me on how good I am on the day – 'We are only as good as the last meal we served' is a good motto for the trainer.

Leaders should be cautious about receiving accolades and deference. Be gracious and don't be fooled. These can be dangerous. Stay real.

### How do you acquire Radar?

Radar is still best acquired in person. Within the City of London, one area is full of banks and another full of insurance companies. This is the way of the traditional market throughout the world, with specialist sections grouped together. This grouping has two functions: not just a specific place for people to buy these products, but also a place where traders can talk and learn from each other. Spending time with contemporaries within your industry is a vital part of Radar activity – people sometimes get deals or new ideas when they pop out for a coffee. If you are located away from such a market hub, find ways through trade fairs, trade association meetings, and even the odd lunch to connect with your industry.

Radar looks outside its own area, too. Innovations in other sectors may later influence yours, so keeping a wider view is important. The internet disrupted many businesses that could have predicted their vulnerability from the damage done to other sectors.

Be prepared to accept radical change. The book *The Black Swan* by Nassim Nicholas Taleb (prophetically published just before the crash of 2008) uses a narrative about a common saying in sixteenth-century England, that something was 'as likely as a black swan', meaning impossible. Then black swans were discovered in Australia and the saying disappeared overnight: people quickly forget their previous beliefs about what was 'impossible'. Taleb points out that very few businesses prepare themselves or protect themselves from huge movements in the market. They seem to assume a straight line of growth, yet if they look back 10, 50 or 100 years, there are countless examples of what Taleb calls Black Swan events – for example, wars, revolutions in technology or recessions – that were not expected and which had devastating consequences.

Also read *The Tipping Point* by Malcolm Gladwell and Joe Girard's *How to Sell Anything to Anybody*.

## The Fox

The Fox is the yang archetype in this Capability Set.

An essential energy in successful leadership is what is called in America 'street smarts'. A naive leader will not last long. Being able to negotiate effectively, to sense when someone is sincere or to spot predators (or, perhaps the most dangerous of all, determined people with good intentions but poor judgement) – these things are essential leadership skills, rarely included in leadership models.

A leader needs to have a nose for a deal. All successful business leaders ultimately ensure that their organisation does lots of profitable business – lots of deals. Sniffing out a deal, on the prowl if you will, enjoying the excitement of finding and winning business – these things are essential. A culture that doesn't revel in seeking out opportunities, that isn't structured to easily take on new projects or customers, is a boring and potentially stagnant one. 'Business either goes up or goes down; it doesn't stay the same'.

The Fox is a survivor. I recently coached the CEO of a division of a French multinational, who told me he was so passionate about his business that to help it survive he would be a 'street fighter'. It sounded strange coming from a smartly dressed, qualified engineer running a division of a corporate business, but I know what he meant. What he was showing was partly Boss energy – the Boss fights for the organisation – but something even more animalistic. He wouldn't just fight; he'd use every trick possible.

Such is the intense energy of the Fox. It is shrewd. It gets what it needs.

I recall a time when we suddenly needed cash and a vindictive bank manager refused to extend our overdraft facility, even though the business was strong. I instigated a sales campaign of some of our smaller assets and offered great prices if people would pay immediately over the phone with credit cards. In 72 hours, we managed to raise three times the amount of the requested overdraft. Now in a position of strength I called the bank's director and told him point blank that a) if he didn't replace this manager, I would leave the bank and b) that I wanted him to personally apologise. The director did apologise and appointed a far more responsive manager as a replacement.

Instinct told me that if I approached the bank with my hand out, pleading, they could have exploited the position and put us into a 'defaulters' division to exploit asset-rich, cash-strapped customers. I had seen this bank do the same to others and I did not want them to have a similar opportunity with my business.

Like the Boss, I know from presenting this material that the Fox is often disliked. Some people find this energy repellent. If people believe the Boss is a bully, the Fox can be seen as a cheat, which for many is far worse. However, as with the Boss, I ask an audience if a leader has no Fox and is naive, if they can't anticipate and protect a business from negative outcomes and can be 'taken to the cleaners' by the vast array of undesirables who will try to take advantage of them, what kind of leader will they be? Clearly, poor.

### The shadow

It is the shadow of the Fox that creates this anxiety: the Crook. This energy is overblown and potentially highly destructive. While the Fox may be suspicious of others' motives, the Crook is paranoid, looking for trouble where there is none. While the Fox understands boundaries, the Crook goes too far.

People who lack Fox energy and who fear being taken advantage of can slip into Crook under the mistaken belief they are being 'streetwise'. They can start overtly challenging people (a Fox would make discreet enquiries). Such Crook behaviour shows real crooks that you are out of your depth. They respect the Fox, however.

Under pressure to succeed, Crook thinking will cross all our minds. However, each one of us has to decide how far we are willing to go to win deals, protect and enrich our business. Such a decision is more complex than conflicting values – it is also about the magnitude of the decision. If the consequence of not pushing the boundaries is huge, how far do you go?

In the section on the Guru, I advised against betting the business. Here, I say 'don't bet yourself'. In the late 1980s, Ernest Saunders, the then CEO of Guinness, colluded with a prominent group of business people to manipulate the stock market value of his company. In 1990, he went to prison for it, and his career was ruined.

### How do you acquire Fox energy?

Honesty is an essential value for human survival, ensuring children keep their parents aware of their behaviours. Trust is key to maintaining lasting relationships and is often people's most important value – whether they are from religious or secular backgrounds. Many cultures also value humility and modesty (especially more conservative ones, where this is often projected onto women). Even in more modern cultures, for both men and women there can be a subtle injunction that you shouldn't show off. Don't be pushy; the tallest daffodil gets its head cut off (a Dutch saying that is repeated in various cultures with different flowers). How can all this be reconciled with the obvious need for a street-smart leader, who can spot predators and will get into a legally defensible scrape to save the business and keep a roof over everyone's head?

For me, the answer is to reframe common perceptions about the Fox. Historically, early societies were structured with a ruler who wanted to have full control. He (it was almost always a 'he') didn't want his army getting 'ideas above their station'. He was going to decide how riches were distributed, although a few merchants were tolerated. Generally, wealth was acquired by violent conquest. If deals were done, he did them, and nobody else.

Dare to stand out, be different, don't be held back by historic beliefs that are irrelevant to the modern business world. These beliefs stop people from learning the skills of sales and marketing. Once these skills are learnt, they have nothing to do with being pushy or dishonest. And without them, you will never become an effective leader.

Read *What They Don't Teach You at Harvard Business School* by Mark McCormack.

## The Friend

The Friend is the yin counterpart to the Fox.

| Conductor | Vision | Character | |
|---|---|---|---|
| | | **Yang** | **Yin** |
| Leadership | Compass | Boss | Coach |
| Operations & Finance | Architect | Express train | |
| **Sales & Marketing** | Radar | Fox | **Friend** |

One of the best salespeople I know has created a dream job of having lunches and meetings with the client pool he personally built up over his career. He tells me that the number of clients he has lost is literally a handful. His business is effectively spending time with a wide group of friends.

The CEO of a leading bank told me that he would only do business with people he liked. 'Life is too short', he said, adding that his experience has been that when he instinctively didn't like someone, they didn't turn into good customers.

My mother always received good service from builders and other tradespeople by developing small personal relationships with them: offering them biscuits or opening up and giving some personal details, raising the relationship beyond the technical to the personal.

The leader needs to be likeable and value building personal relationships.

People feel valued if you show some interest in who they are and what is important to them. I once had a long conversation about the wonders of Microsoft Excel with an accountant. He was truly excited by how this tool works. I was less excited, but I shared his enthusiasm. Showing genuine interest in someone beyond the job in hand, even a smile or a positive acknowledgement – these create relationships. At some level, this is being charming. Some people equate this with being manipulative. I don't. It's just the Friend archetype in action – pleasant and professional.

A coaching technique from NLP called 'Matching and Mirroring' can help bring the Friend into play. This involves discretely copying someone's body language, especially gestures: according to NLP, copying the rhythm and micro-movements of someone while you are communicating creates a sense of connection.

I needed to find a new key supplier for the business, as our main existing one had imposed terms that were uncommercial. At a critical meeting, I met a director of one of these companies. I barely spoke, just copied his hand gestures (I moved my hands under the meeting room table to do this). At one point, he suddenly jumped up, held out his hand and said, 'I know we have a deal'. We did, and we still do almost eight years later.

Although this may seem somewhat contrived, I had a sincere intention to authentically connect with this person. People are not fools and they will sense if you are insincere or trying to manipulate them.

New leaders need to start building an informal advisory team, a network of trusted contacts and mentors who will advise them on complex issues.

If you are currently working within an organisation, that is the best place to start this 'team-building'. Many experts in various parts of it will be delighted to explain procedures, as they are enthusiastic for others to buy in to their approaches. This creates a double win for you; first, you will have new contacts and allies, and second, your business knowledge will grow. The modern company can be like a university if you know how to use it as one.

Modern organisations are keen on mentoring; senior people will expect to be asked to take 'rising stars' under their wing. Asking potential mentors to play this role for you is well worth doing.

The informal networks that leaders create can often be more powerful than any official one. A headmaster I worked with left to go to a new school and brought many of the best teachers with him. A CEO I know sold a business and a couple of years later started a new one, whereupon his old colleagues quit their jobs and joined him. Large companies that acquire smaller ones often find, to their frustration, that even decades later the informal networks are still alive and well from those original companies. A leader often creates a 'clan' that will stick together through thick and thin. Part of this is Coach energy, but much of it is the Friend, building relationships that can last a lifetime. Spending that extra time to get to know someone can be one of the best investments a leader can make.

A network also provides protection. Sadly, even the most able people can find themselves working for unpleasant bosses. They generally will steal your glory, but in the worst cases, such bosses can set about damaging your reputation as they may perceive you as a threat. You need allies in these scenarios.

### The shadow

The shadow of the Friend is the Creep. A common human trait is to find ourselves in a negative state in social situations (bringing back awkward memories from childhood or adolescence). This is added to in the business world by maxims like 'It's not what you know, it's who you know' or 'You only get one chance to make a first impression'.

My sense of my own Creep energy is that when I feel stressed in a social situation I become something like a dismissive adolescent. I often use humour, as I was a class clown as a teenager. This can work at times, but can also be inappropriate. People tend to revert to early coping strategies when under this type of stress. Some go into their shell. Others push themselves forward too much. What is your own? Most of these behaviours are ultimately driven by a sense of shame: 'I don't belong'.

At one level, the answer is simple: have the courage to be you. I did my first public presentation in my early 40s and now I am teaching people how to be presenters and trainers. Although I had a natural aptitude at public speaking, I still found the experience stressful: apparently public speaking is commonly one of the most frightening experiences. It took me many years to stop being funny and have enough belief in myself to simply be me.

Having a philosophy that stresses one's own independence can lessen the sense of social pressure that brings out the Creep. A doctor I know made frequent appearances on breakfast television when it was first introduced in the UK and attracted audiences of millions. I asked her, 'Weren't you nervous?' She replied, 'What's the worst that could happen? At the end of the day, my motto is "I just don't give a damn"'.

Office politics is often seen as the hunting ground for the Creep, who can hold the belief that *all* that is needed for success is to ingratiate themselves with influential people.

As I have said, creating a network is part of building a career. Understanding the difference between the Friend and the Creep will help you do this in a positive way that earns respect.

### How do you acquire the Friend?

It is not easy to change your character, but it is easier to change your beliefs about the world. Having a belief that you and others will win can have a profound effect on you. People do not always behave well, but rather than be disappointed, if you set out to win and want them to win too, then you can simply walk away if something doesn't work out – no hard feelings. Such an approach, the 'win-win' model of Game Theory, is what the Friend is all about: entering into negotiations with the positive attitude that either both parties win or you politely walk away and only come back when win-win is on the table.

One alternative is a *win-lose* approach. In its most aggressive form, this is a Genghis Khan philosophy: 'It's not enough for me to win; I must also see you lose'. More common is a desire to win and an indifference as to what happens to others. Being a winner in business is a good thing, but when this is consistently done at other people's expense, it will ruin the chances of repeat customers and recommendations. Although business can be a bit 'rough and tumble', when you set out to do business in such a way that both parties win, you can form lasting relationships that are far more beneficial than those that result from the 'eat what you kill then move on to the next' approach. I also believe that if you are doing business with competent people who are also winners, you have higher quality customers. If you have a win-lose mindset, your market will be restricted to people you can get one over on.

The opposite of this is a *lose-win* approach, behind which lies a prevailing lack of self-belief, a conviction that you are somehow a fraud and others will detect it in you. People with this mindset may learn all the Friend's influencing skills, but use them simply to hide behind a mask, while retaining a sense 'this isn't me'. Low self-esteem may seem more admirable than conceit, but it often leads to the same presentation: forcing you to be fake. If you practice lose-win, you will end up resenting the other party and often find unconscious ways of taking revenge on the winner. This is a destructive pattern. If you embrace wanting to win yourself, you paradoxically become more generous and more likely to want others to win too.

The book *A Course in Miracles* states, that ultimately, we can either make decisions coming from a place of *love* or a place of *fear*.

This goes back to the leader's personal compass. Do we choose to believe the world is fundamentally abundant so that win-win can be the basis of all our relationships? Or do we choose to believe that the world is fundamentally hostile and there isn't enough pie to go around? The interesting thing is that neither of these views is 'true'. The world is complex. However, if we choose to believe that it is abundant, then a very different, and I would argue more inspiring, way of leading both ourselves and others will emerge. This is not to say that there aren't bad things and exploitative people out there – there are, and that is exactly why the leader needs Fox energy, to balance the Friend and ensure the leader is abundant but not naive.

## Stepping up to leadership from sales and marketing

Like leaders stepping up from any other function, former sales and marketing specialists have to let go of their need to 'do the work' and ensure that their original function is handled well by others. Key relationships can be maintained, by an occasional meal or some other form of entertainment, but the actual sales function needs to be delegated to others. Most successful sales people like people and developing relationships – the secret is to map that across to a passion for *internal* relationships, creating time to mentor and guide their team. Some of the strength of the Fox becomes the more direct and boundaried Boss. The 'them' of Radar is expanded to include the 'we' of the Compass. The Friend can develop into the Coach.

At some level, this transition into leadership skills can be made quite easily and elegantly. However, sales can have a deferential approach – the professional sales person will tactfully ignore aspects of their customer's behaviour, as they are not there to teach their customer but to earn from them. Leadership requires a paradigm shift to where expressing your values and asserting boundaries is not just desirable but essential. A continued fear of rejection, natural in the sales process, will undermine your authority. Leaders can't always please people; they need to do the right thing.

The sales person moving up to leadership needs to build a strong Architect, Express Train and Alarm Bell too. This requires time spent understanding and learning from operations and finance people.

An important shift is to move from a turnover mentality to a profit one: 'Turnover is vanity, profits are sanity'.

The sales metaphor of the oil pipeline demonstrates the power a sales person can deploy when sales is properly integrated into finance and operations. The pipeline requires two key processes to take place: drilling and refining. Sales activity is like the process of prospecting land and investing in test drilling until oil is struck. Each oil well represents a customer. A pipeline is built connecting these wells to the refinery, where the oil is distilled into various end products. The refinery represents operations. If there is too oil much pouring out of the wells, the refinery is overwhelmed and oil needs to be stored, which is also potentially dangerous. If there is not enough oil, the refinery doesn't cover its costs and puts the entire business in danger. The job of a leader is to ensure a number of things: that there is a good system that maintains a consistent flow down the pipeline, so the refinery is working at optimum capacity; that new refining capacity is built to cope with expansion of the number and output of the wells (or cut back if there are significant falls); and that a good financial buffer is in place to ensure that there is both enough money to pay for new drilling and refineries and enough 'fat' to wait for these to start paying their way. Such is the oil business, and such, actually, is all business. What an exciting metaphor for a sales person (or anyone) to see this great machine actually do what they want: sustainably making more money and consistently delivering satisfaction to the customer.

## The balance of the three

With the right level of Radar, Fox and Friend, a leader has creative vision, intuits what the customer wants, builds solid relationships and avoids time wasters or worse. This Capability Set transcends the role of sales; it is needed for leaders in all kinds of organisations, not just commercial ones – the armed forces, local government, health care, political parties and so on.

When these qualities lack balance, things are not so good.

If you have Radar and Fox and lack Friend, you would be like a shark. You won't be able to maintain a steady of flow of customers. Salespeople are sometimes described as hunters or farmers – to me success is being able to do both: hunt for new customers and then farm them for a steady flow of ongoing business. Hunting only is effectively 'kill, eat and move on', a primitive form of business.

If you have Radar and Friend and lack Fox, you will be taken advantage of by others who will steal your glory.

If you have Fox and Friend and no Radar, you will continue selling horses and carts and become irrelevant.

## Conclusion

These nine archetypes and their shadows are, I believe, the essential elements that a leader needs to have at their disposal. But simply having them is not enough. To lead, you need to be able to use them appropriately: the right one, in the right measure, at the right time.

That is what the next part of the book is about.

# Shadows

In the preceding chapters, I described how every archetype has a shadow. Here are some general points about shadows and how to manage them.

As I mentioned in the introduction, enjoying the benefits of an archetype that 'shines brightly' means learning to live with the consequences of the greater shadow that is cast. I have a gift of being action orientated (I have a strong Express Train); I have had to learn to manage this, otherwise my life can flip between Steam Roller and Headless Chicken, which is very stressful. This is probably why I have gained expertise in mindfulness to manage my own shadows. Others with the great gift of the Coach often have to learn to manage the emotional pain that goes with the gift of sensitivity and intuition. Understanding your own unique gifts and learning to manage the resulting shadows can be truly life changing.

Becoming curious about our responses, rather than letting them dominate us, is a key leadership quality. Our shadows often have very useful information for us: they are a calling for us to face the parts we need to develop, which we tend to ignore. They can also motivate us to create new strategies to better manage ourselves and become more self-reflective. They are a powerful signal of our unmet needs. Learn to accept your shadows, rather than feeling shame, disowning or repressing them.

Play to your weaknesses. Often shadows emerge by using the 'wrong' archetype for the situation. If someone is conflict-avoidant and finds a *yang* archetype a challenge, they may appear as a *yin* shadow, a victim or a manipulator, in compensation. It is better to apply the appropriate archetype to the situation, even if it is a personal challenge, than to fall back upon a more comfortable area and use its shadow.

When a strong stress response has been triggered (see Chapter 6), it can be far more difficult to contain our shadows. At these times, detach yourself so you don't say something you may later regret.

Shadows trigger other people's shadows (and other people's shadows trigger ours). The famous author and psychologist Herman Hesse wrote: 'If you hate a person, you hate something in him that is part of yourself. What isn't part of ourselves doesn't disturb us'.

This is particularly true of shadows – but it can actually work in two ways. If I feel ashamed of a shadow in myself, I can find someone irritating and hard to lead if they share that shadow. But there are also people I feel drawn to, whom I later realise share a shadow with me, one that I tolerate and secretly quite like.

A key leadership skill is judging character. Is someone trustworthy or not? The danger is that one can mistake these shadow-driven likes and dislikes with objective judgements about trustworthiness and competence. We can be fooled by someone untrustworthy with whom we enjoy sharing a shadow. We can push aside someone who, although they share a shadow of ours that we feel ashamed of, is actually reliable. Know the difference between a negative intuition about someone and an unfounded personal prejudice: understanding your own shadows can be the key to this.

# Part II

# The tenth element: mindfulness

Using the right element at the right time

# 5 The Conductor

| | Vision | Character | |
|---|---|---|---|
| | | Yang | Yin |
| **Conductor** | | | |
| **Leadership** | Compass | Boss | Coach |
| **Operations & Finance** | Architect | Express train | Alarm bell |
| **Sales & Marketing** | Radar | Fox | Friend |

Back to the Steve Jobs movie and his quote from it: 'I play the orchestra'. This is the next evolution of the business leader, a change of their identity from a specialist to a generalist who can access all the nine archetypal energies.

However, as I have said, it is not enough just to have the ability to access the nine archetypes. They need to be brought to bear *at the right time*. This is the purpose of the tenth and arguably most important archetype in my model, the Conductor.

The Conductor is, in a sense, a space you enter to form a 'helicopter view' of all the other archetypes. It starts with clearing one's mind. I find the best way to do this is to simply pause and briefly use a mindfulness technique (covered in Part III). After a minute or so, I can then reconsider the issue at hand, and can explore all the other archetypes to determine a course of action.

You are probably already aware which of the archetype(s) is *your* preferred space to 'hang out' in, especially under pressure. It is generally this one that needs to be kept in check. As I have mentioned, I automatically leap to Express Train (or Steamroller). This isn't always helpful. I have learnt that when I feel the need to take action, I ensure that I make a brief detour to the Conductor, to enable me to consider other options first.

A business decision is likely to be a sequence of archetypes (and potential shadows) managed by the Conductor. I will use the following example: a meeting with an individual you are considering promoting.

You like them (Friend energy) and know they have the right experience (a rational, structured Architect conclusion). But as the two of you converse, you notice that their body language seems somewhat uncontrolled. Your Fox becomes curious at this. Time to move into the Conductor. Here, all the archetypes have space to 'speak up'. You get a sense from your Boss that the person is trustworthy: they're not shifting about because they are trying to deceive you, but for some other reason, probably nerves. Your Coach energy is then brought to the fore – they will need some training to become more confident and self-aware. But the Architect can organise that; this slight nervousness is no barrier to their doing the job well. The Conductor 'asks' – do they get the job? There is a 'yes' (the moment of decision is highly personal and that 'yes' may not be in words). The Conductor then 'asks' if any of the other archetypes have any objection? There is silence. In offering them the job, you use your Compass to inspire them with the spirit that the work requires – what it is truly in service of. Your Coach also advises them that part of their development for the new role will involve further training.

Without the Conductor and then the Coach, your original Fox curiosity could have turned into a Steamroller (shoot first and ask questions later) and turned aggressive and inappropriate (Bully and Psychoanalyst), forcefully pointing out the inappropriate body language and turning the interview into a confrontation. The key point here is to allow the Conductor to broaden the argument, taking it beyond a single dimension.

My experience during the credit crunch provides another example of the Conductor at work. I began the story in the section on the Alarm Bell in Chapter 3, when I asked the staff member to remove the one big sale and the forecast graph suddenly plummeted into an impending cash crisis. Now it continues.

After the Alarm Bell started ringing, my next response was fairly aggressive. I felt the Bully and Steamroller rising within me – I said to myself, 'This is an emergency! I want action now!' I spotted this and went into the Conductor, where I knew I needed to activate the Compass in the long term, but right now I needed a touch of Fox not to panic everyone else. Using some Coach energy, in a pleasant way I said, 'OK, let me go away and think about this – let's meet again after lunch', and brought the meeting tactfully to a close.

Back in my office, a few moments of calm in Conductor led me to visit the Compass. What was the vision now? It didn't take long to work that out: survive! The Alarm Bell and Architect suggested I quickly find out how much of a cash buffer was needed for the next three months. My Express Train was raring to go, but I reassembled the team after lunch and we agreed an action plan.

We would need to shift into winter mode. We initiated a redundancy program, which I carried out with a heavy heart. Once this had been done, I took time out in Compass, to consider where we go from here. It was not easy – Radar was telling me that there was no short-term fix to the financial system; the recession meant that each day brought more unsettling news; the situation was deteriorating at a fast pace. The next few years were full of winter experiences.

I busily attempted to restore the business, but nothing lasting could happen in such an unstable economic environment. Trying to agree deals with troubled organisations (who weren't actually interested in doing any business) meant ongoing negotiations with no conclusion. Exhausting as this was, it did keep the 'door open'. I used all the archetypes to survive this fruitless negotiation roundabout and my Conductor helped me detach. It took four years to find a new positive Compass.

Looking back, I am painfully aware of my own shadows and how at times I let myself act from them. The Steamroller in not taking enough time to oversee key decisions. A lack of Boss for not sticking to my guns at times. The Psychoanalyst in justifying my own conflict avoidance by playing 'coach'. The Crook in being somehow attracted to people's shadow qualities (and being in denial about this). The Bully and Headless Chicken – overdoing my outrage and pushing people around.

## The Matrix Coach

I would like to generalise the above examples so you can apply them in any business context. What follows is a quick, practical way of using the entire Matrix to assist you in making a business decision, or to help you work out next steps in any situation when you are unsure what to do next.

a   First, start in Conductor by pausing for a few moments, to relax yourself. Simply focus on your breathing. When you feel a bit calmer, return to the issue at hand.

b   Using the graphic below, 'visit' each of the archetypes, I suggest you start with Compass and then move to Boss, Coach, Architect (and so on) – but this is for guidance only. The order is up to your own personal taste.

c   Consider the issue from the perspective of each archetype and let your Conductor simply listen.

d   Visit all the archetypes. The Conductor has a key role in ensuring you visit each one and don't stop midway if you feel you already have the answer. Keep going.

e   Once you have finished, notice any archetypes that 'stuck out' then use your Conductor to orchestrate an internal conversation between the various archetypes to thrash the issue out.

| Conductor | Vision | Character | |
|---|---|---|---|
| | | **Yang** | **Yin** |
| **Leadership** | Compass | Boss | Coach |
| **Operations & Finance** | Architect | Express train | Alarm bell |
| **Sales & Marketing** | Radar | Fox | Friend |

Here are some useful questions you may wish to use with each archetype, after you have initially settled into the Conductor:

| Compass | – What is this in service of? |
|---|---|
| Boss | – Am I being pressured? |
| Coach | – Will this make my life (other's lives) more pleasant / easier? |
| Architect | – Will this outcome undermine our overall system? |
| Express Train | – Is there a rush? |
| Alarm Bell | – Could it create any problems? |
| Radar | – Is this the right time given my expectations of the market? |
| Fox | – Am I getting ripped off? Can I trust this person (people)? |
| Friend | – What can I do to make a better connection with the people involved? |

After these questions, I sit in Conductor and reflect on the answers. This sets off other questions, until I reach a conclusion for the next step.

After teaching this model for many years, I have found that people can, after practicing for a while, simply take a deep breath then look at the graphic and discuss the issue from the different perspectives.

You may find that one archetype 'shouts loudest' (or that a few do). Your Conductor ensures that you don't lose your focus and, instead, remain detached and simply notice the intensity of any particular archetype without either pushing it away or embracing it.

Once you have considered the situation from each archetype's perspective, you remain in your Conductor, but now with the intention of reaching a decision. You can continue the discussion with the archetypes you have identified as pivotal for this decision. The Conductor will eventually either know what to do or realise that more time and information are needed.

In Appendix B, I cover a more structured way of doing this, using the NLP technique of anchoring. I call this the 'NLP Matrix Coach'.

## The Conductor and a new sense of self

The Conductor provides an evolution to a new sense of self – that of a generalist leader.

In my mid-20s, I decided to 'live the dream' of my teenage years and become a professional drummer – I gave up my job in the computer industry. I joined a serious band and spent each day rehearsing and doing gigs and recordings. I began to see myself as a professional musician. But two things happened in short succession that ended my aspiring career. First, I began to have doubts about the band leader's ability to 'make it'. I was effectively taking a poorly paid job working for a boss who might not actually have what it takes (I hope that if my boss had been Sting, I would have known it and stuck around). Second, I went to see a performance by Steve Gadd, arguably the best drummer in the world. Watching him play, I felt he was almost a different species from me.

I decided to go into business instead, because I wanted to have a financially comfortable life. I recall telling a friend at the time: 'As a musician, you have to be world class to guarantee any success; as a business person, your success is directly proportional to your ability: a reasonable business person will at least make reasonable money'. I then started a business, using my computer skills in a niche property sector. I had become a de facto business leader, but I still saw myself as a computer expert.

The business grew slowly and I started employing people. A key point came when I stopped programming, delegated those tasks and concentrated on running the business as a whole. I now realised I was a business leader. After that the business truly flourished.

The purpose of this story is that it shows two pivotal stages in our working life.

Very few people in their childhood want a career in business; most children dream of a more prestigious or celebrity-style life. The first pivotal point comes when we sacrifice our dreams to become a specialist.

Acquiring a specialism to a competent level generally takes about five years. After ten years some people really excel and are ready to harvest their talents. At this point, perhaps in their early to mid-30s, they have 'arrived' – a good salary and some of the trappings of success. They continue to work in the same way and get more and more rewarded. However, another five years on, they can become stale: people in their late 30s to early 40s will need to move up, or they are likely to enter a comfort zone where over the following years they will begin to deteriorate. Therefore, good companies will promote their rising stars after ten or 15 years in work, to ensure they have a productive future.

This is the point at which I hear many people say, 'I like my job, now I am good at it. But they don't want me to do it anymore; they want me to manage people, which I don't like. I just want to get on with my work'. In some fields, it can be possible to continue 'working'. Some partnerships classify their partners as 'finders', 'minders' and 'grinders', where finders (the best rewarded) find new clients and new deals, minders look after the clients and grinders, highly specialised virtuosos, do the actual work. However, in most hierarchical organisations, specialists will generally be encouraged to move up to a management role or to move out. This means a shift of identity, a second pivotal change.

This is where the Conductor becomes essential. It helps you let go of your specialisation and gives you space to move your attention to new areas.

Leadership is a decision, a decision to view the world as a generalist, as a Conductor: wanting to develop our missing talents and finding ways of doing so.

## How do you learn the Conductor?

The Matrix Coach (and the NLP Matrix Coach in Appendix B) are useful ways to learn the Conductor and have a 'one-to-one' with each archetype. It will help you 'inhabit' those you have previously ignored. As you become more experienced, you will find yourself changing your energy to the appropriate archetype instinctively.

However, I believe there is one essential key to acquiring a powerful and effective Conductor. That is the practice of mindfulness.

# 6 Mindfulness

Mindfulness is a mental state, where your conscious attention is taken up with experiencing the present moment. You are no longer dominated by your thoughts and feelings; you have a choice whether to engage with them or not. You become an 'observer' of your thoughts and feelings.

Mindfulness is also an attitude. It is a different way of experiencing life: making a conscious choice to actively engage in the experience of the present moment rather than to spend your time projecting your thoughts and feelings into the future or past.

From a leadership perspective, mindfulness helps you to be far more aware of what is going on around you. Likewise, you become more aware of the signals you send others (and gain far greater awareness of your own internal signals and what they are trying to tell you).

Mindfulness is a skill. Like any other skill, it needs practice. A useful, formal way of practice is to meditate. Part III of this book is a workbook with suggested meditation exercises. I strongly advise you to try these and discover the benefits for yourself. Meditation, by the way, is not itself mindfulness; it is a way of getting to mindfulness.

You can learn to enter the mindful state in a matter of moments. About 20 years ago, I attended a yoga and meditation course given by an elderly gentleman called Billy Doyle in his small flat in Hampstead in North London. I recall one time he entered the room and sat down on his mat with an earnest intensity. He rolled his eyes, closed them and seemed immediately to go into a state of peace and mindfulness. This was an 'A-ha' moment for me, as I realised that you didn't need to sit in silence for ages to enter this state. Instead, once you have discovered it within yourself and have learnt how to enter it, the state is always available for you.

Finally, mindfulness is an aesthetic value that is worth cultivating: fully appreciating what you are experiencing right now. That could be enjoying looking at a beautiful painting, enjoying your food while eating, feeling the warm water on your hands while washing, noticing the sensations in your mouth while brushing your teeth, enjoying walking or any activity, whatever it may be.

Part of mindfulness is noticing when you are *not* mindful – that you are not fully engaged with what you are doing at the moment and are instead lost in thought. When you have this realisation, you then decide to switch your focus back to being fully present. It would be torturous to do this every waking moment, but even the occasional switch back into the moment can be very worthwhile.

Here are some benefits of mindfulness:

1    Stress management. Mindfulness has been shown to switch off the adrenalin gland, the hormone that produces the stress response, and instead bring about what is called the 'relaxation response'. Once you become experienced at practicing mindfulness, you are also able to relax much more quickly and efficiently. This enables you to avoid indulging in negative addictive behaviours.

---

### The stress response

For mammals (and thus humans), the stress response has evolved to deal with danger. It has proven remarkably effective. When we are in danger, the adrenalin gland in our lower back pumps out the hormone and puts us in a state of readiness. Blood flows into the limbs, so we can be ready to fight, flee or freeze. It is taken from the digestive system and, most interestingly, from our frontal cortex (where humans think). Sadly, this system designed for mammals shuts off part of our newly evolved human thinking brain. This is why a key task of a leader is to be sufficiently self-aware that they don't make major decisions during a time of intense personal stress, as they literally don't have access to all their faculties.

In his book *The Chimp Paradox*, Dr Steve Peters describes this process as our 'human' being taken over by our 'chimp'.

For more on this topic, read *The Relaxation Response* by Herbert Benson, Professor of Mind/Body Medicine at Harvard Medical School.

---

2    Mindfulness builds resilience. For leadership, this quality changes from becoming desirable to essential: a true test of the mettle of leader is how they respond in a crisis. Mindfulness builds the resilience muscle so that when a crisis comes you are not running near empty and you have reserves of energy.
3    Mindfulness helps us overcome habitual negative patterns of thought. Leaders are thinkers – but can get trapped in their thoughts (paralysis by analysis). Mindfulness enables you to detach yourself from thought, so that you become an observer of your mind at work. You can begin to categorise your thoughts into helpful and unhelpful. The unhelpful ones are often well-worn grooves where you habitually worsen your mood with overly negative projections of the future or bad memories from the past.

Mindfulness enables you to notice this type of thinking and to choose to not engage with it.

4 As your attention changes, you can focus onto the type of thinking you are doing, rather than the content of those thoughts. When I have a problem with someone, I tend to replay what I intend to say to them over and over again – this could keep me awake at night. Now, I catch myself doing this and say to myself, 'Do I have a workable first step?' If yes, I then notice the thoughts starting again, but rather than engage with them, this time I watch the pattern replaying and have a choice to do something different. Mindfulness doesn't mean stopping yourself thinking – that would be impossible. It is a subtle change of focus to an awareness of the *type* of thinking you are doing.

5 Building creativity. According to neuroscientist Richard Davidson, mindfulness actually energises and reprograms the part of the brain responsible for imagination and forward thinking. Modern neurology is moving away from the idea that the brain is physically fixed, towards the notion of plasticity, that its structure can change.

6 Davidson also argues that mindfulness reduces the often excessive avoidant energy from the right side of the brain. People who become experts in a field prior to leadership may have been trained to be highly risk averse. A condition detrimental to leadership can evolve: loss aversion, where people become so fearful of loss that they are unable to use the key qualities of will, creativity and imagination. Mindfulness can help restore this natural balance.

7 Creating charisma. There is an interesting ambiguity around the words 'present' and 'presence'. Leaders are often described as people who are larger than life, who fill a room – i.e. they have personal *presence*. However, mindfulness is the practice of becoming *present*, fully 'in the room' right now. It is no coincidence that these two words are so similar. When someone listens to you with full attention, not distracted by their own thoughts or agenda but listening to you with interest and curiosity, this person is listening with presence and, I would argue, *has* presence. Former US President Bill Clinton was reportedly like this: people who met him felt he had been particularly pleased to meet them and was genuinely interested in their story.

8 Goal realisation. Mindfulness helps positive visualisation. Great athletes, such as tennis champion Novak Djokovic, use visualisation to mentally rehearse success. Part of this process involves stilling the mind beforehand, to produce a 'blank canvas' where this visualisation can take place. Alternatively, mindfulness can silence negative thoughts that can make athletes choke. Usain Bolt, currently the world's fastest man, was asked what he did before he ran. He simply said, 'I just try and relax'.

9 Improved performance. When I exercise (especially stretching afterwards) and while I swim, I take the trouble to really focus on relaxing and being aware of the subtle movements in different parts of my body.

My performance has improved greatly as a result, and I enjoy the activity more, too.

## Mindfulness and the archetypes

### Vision

The word vision implies something to do with your eyes, but in this context, it means a sense of something in the future. This doesn't need to be visual; sounds, feelings or words are fine too. For the Compass, create a positive inner representation of something you can metaphorically move towards. For Architect, imagine what a new product or process might look, sound or feel like. For Radar, imagine what people would want and what a specific customer might look like, say or feel if they were satisfied with your product or service. Imagine the effects that these satisfied customers would have on the wider market. All of these things help you plan and prepare for what is important. As sports people know, it actually increases your chances of success. If you can imagine something, it is more likely to happen.

### Yin

Mindfulness boosts sensitivity and intuition: the qualities of the *yin* column of the Matrix. For the Coach, Alarm Bell and Friend, mindfulness helps you become aware of your own feelings and intuitions, in order to build and maintain a good quality of connection with other people. This sensitivity also helps you become aware of a connection to yourself – as author and trainer Richard Moss says, 'The distance between you and another person is the same as the distance between you and yourself'. Developing a clear awareness of our own inner state enables a closer connection to other people. It is additionally a very useful form of personal management – you can track which things affect you and work out what you can do differently. It also prevents you from slipping into shadows.

The word *boundaries* has become very popular. It means creating some rules of conduct, developing adequate self-control and protection, and learning to express your needs clearly. There are two main forms of boundaries, inner and outer. An outer boundary is created by expression, clearly asserting your needs and stopping another person from bullying or overwhelming you. An inner boundary is containment, maintaining your cool and not 'spilling out' your heated emotions onto others. There is an important interaction between the inner and outer boundaries when people are stressed. Some people over-express and can intimidate others, when more containment is required, for instance the Bully. Other people tend to bottle things up with too much containment and not enough expression, for instance the Creep. Or they bottle things up then suddenly lash out during a 'last straw' scenario (suddenly flipping to Bully). The desired state is to have a good interaction and balance between both our inner and outer boundaries, so we can both express and contain as required. However, each of us will tend to veer towards too much expression or too much containment. This is where mindfulness helps. By being aware of our own pattern, we can enter Conductor and choose to express ourselves ('Don't back down now') or choose to contain ('Live to fight another day'), judging the moment.

Authenticity means expression. The constantly calculating business leader, who never expresses themselves or their passion, can seem lifeless, manipulative and unattractively scary. Anger gets a bad rap, but sometimes expressing yourself forcefully without losing control shows what your 'worst' looks like. If you never show this, people may fear that your 'worst' could be truly terrible.

### *Yang*

The *yang* column of the Matrix is associated with the Warrior energy mentioned in Chapter 2. This may sound a bit masculine or aggressive, but it is part of everyone's make-up and, as I said, is as much about stillness as action. Meditation is a key part of the eastern tradition of warrior training, which has evolved into the softer versions of yoga, Tai Chi and seated practice. The Warrior first needs to be still and fully focused, not overwhelmed by fear but aware of it. Eckhart Tolle likens this energy to a cat sitting by a mouse hole, waiting for the mouse to emerge. The cat is fully present, ready to pounce, yet its body is relaxed.

Martial artist and psychologist Tony Felix points out that historically armies would spend months, if not years, marching home from war. This would give them the chance of cleansing themselves from the horrors of battle. The modern soldier often flies home, arriving in a family situation hours after combat, making that adjustment far more difficult. Although less extreme, at certain points in business, a leader will call upon a lot of Boss energy, and some degree of Bully will, most likely, be activated too. These energies need to dissipate after they have been used. Cardiovascular exercise can certainly help this release, but one can remain quite 'pumped' immediately after exercise. Meditation is an alternative way of rapidly releasing the adrenalin so you can return home to your family or handle more delicate work situations after time in Warrior mode.

During periods of peace, Eastern warriors would spend hours each day meditating, keeping their mind sharp and avoiding boredom and drunken brawls. The stillness that meditation brings enabled these ancient warriors to keep their battle skills sharp. There is something counter-intuitive that such a peaceful practice can be of such help in preparing for the most powerful and dangerous of human encounters: battle.

Looking at the yang archetypes in more detail, mindful practice enables us to stay in them without straying into their shadows. Let me give a few examples:

*Boss*. I am having a heated telephone conversation with someone and notice that my shoulders are hunched and the volume of my voice has increased. I am simultaneously having this conversation and am mindfully aware of my state during it. I notice that I am slipping into Bully. I push the mute button briefly, take a deep breath – Aaaah – and go into the Conductor. What is the best next step? Answer: briefly summarise my concerns and end the call fairly quickly. I am back to a grounded Boss energy. Off goes the mute, and the conversation resumes in a proper business-like manner.

*Express Train.* I sense I am becoming overwhelmed and slipping into Steamroller during a meeting. Another quiet deep breath enables me to reconnect with my Conductor. What is the best next step? Answer: to agree the next action point with the person responsible and bring this section to a close. I am calm and clear again.

*Fox.* I am introduced to a potential supplier and my Fox doesn't trust him. I slip into Crook and start cornering him intellectually, trying to publicly humiliate him to show he isn't a 'good egg'. I sense something is wrong, and take a deep breath and go into Conductor. I become aware of what is going on. I ask, what is the best course of action right now? To bring the meeting politely and pleasantly to a close. I then need to meet with the relevant people in the team and say in Boss mode that we will not be doing business with this individual and that my decision is final.

### Mindfulness and the Conductor

The Conductor is mindfulness in action, with one important difference.

Both the practice of mindfulness and accessing the Conductor start with an initial pause – taking a few moments to chill out, reflect and settle yourself. You take a brief break from whatever is preoccupying you at that moment so you can enter the helicopter view (you can't 'take off' until your mind is fairly settled).

The similarity continues as you follow a pre-set mental process to explore something from different perspectives. In the mindful state, you choose not to engage with the thoughts you notice. The Conductor, however, does engage, briefly, letting them have their say but then choosing to move on to the next archetype in the sequence.

## Conclusion

Mindfulness provides the gateway to the Conductor, so you can rise above your instincts under pressure and create new choices for more productive behaviour. However, there is also something deeper about the practice. Mindfulness and meditation are fundamentally about believing that a part of you exists that is not your thoughts or feelings but which can observe those thoughts and feelings. This part is friendly and consistent, and is sometimes referred to as the higher self.

My own experience of this is when I have truly connected to, and inhabit this silent space, I have a sense of a connection to my true wisdom. I trust it more than any of the other archetypes to make the right decision – it is my internal leader, my Conductor.

# 7 Superconductor

## Using the Matrix in your organisation

The principal idea behind this chapter is that once the leader has developed an understanding of the Matrix for themselves, this internal understanding can be transferred as a diagnostic for the organisation (or unit) they lead.

Managers delegate tasks; leaders delegate functions. The job of leadership is first to find someone to lead each of the core functions, then to move into what I call a Superconductor space, where weakness in these departments (and thus in the overall system) can be detected and improved. You become the 'health monitor' of your organisation. I know some great leaders who can simply walk around their premises for 20 minutes and know if something is wrong – this is the instinctive Superconductor.

Organisations, like people, tend to have personalities (or cultures), and sometimes skewed ones. Often these can be traced back to the personalities of the original founders. When an organisation lacks Express Train or Boss, it lacks decisiveness. With too much Boss and not enough Coach, it can become 'dog eat dog'. The more time people in an organisation spend protecting themselves from negative aspects of these cultures, the less productive the organisation becomes.

However, cultures can be notoriously difficult to change. I worked as a coach in a leading regional bank whose new owners had brought in a modern, 'thrusting' CEO to shake up the old guard. When the credit crunch came, the old guard thrust him out, and the culture shifted right back to where it had started. Had it ever really changed?

One way to find out if a culture has changed is to pose as a customer for your own business. Check if it is really good at taking on new customers. Test this in various ways. Telephone your own business; does anyone answer the phone (and if so, after how many rings)? When someone does answer, are they friendly? Email your business; how quick and thorough is the response? Is there a timely follow-up? Challenge the sales and operations functions to explain how elegantly they can take on a significant new customer – are there sufficient people and resources in place to do this, or is everyone so overwhelmed (or culturally stuck) that new customers are seen as a nuisance? Ask the function leader what their plans are to put top of their game teams and elegant processes in place. Are they up to the job? What are their constraints? The leader needs to champion changes of practices – and spot the weaknesses. Is there a big enough marketing or staff budget?

This same approach is also needed for new products.

Once a leader catalyses a change in a department, the system may go out of balance and people can try to undermine progress. That is why leaders need to monitor all aspects of the system in this championing.

At the same time, the leader mustn't go into Steamroller and flatten everybody. Leaders have to learn when to push the system and when to give it time to catch up. The Conductor, as always, is at the heart of making such judgements.

Robert Dilts interviewed an artist who worked for Walt Disney during the period when feature length cartoons such as Snow White and Bambi were taking the world by storm. The artist explained that there were 'three Walts', and you never knew which one would show up at a meeting. He could be a dreamer, highly imaginative and positive. He could be a realist, very practical. Or he could be a spoiler, who was very critical and scary. Though the team never knew which one would show up, after a meeting everyone seemed to agree that the 'right' Walt had been there, even though this was often very disconcerting. Disney must have had a powerful and intuitive Conductor, which 'told him who to be' at any given moment.

I use the Matrix model to lead a board of directors. Sometimes I sense one or more of them is in a comfort zone and needs some Compass to inspire them to think bigger. I may also use some Boss energy to challenge this comfort zone and clearly express my expectations that they will step up. At other times, they seem very passionate or upset about some issue, and it is best for me to listen very attentively in Coach mode.

If we are discussing a problem or a new opportunity, I will go into Coach and ask questions inspired by other archetypes. For instance, when the issue is around operations, I would use Architect: 'Please let me know what specific plans you have to make this happen and when'. For sales, I may ask a similar question around a marketing plan, or I may ask them to use Friend more and actually take a customer or supplier out to lunch or meet with them some other way. I am using the Matrix model to manage the energies within the team, providing challenge and inspiration if something is wrong or is slowing progress.

However, there is a creative tension here – if I want to have a team of genuine leaders of their departments and/or functions, I have to let them do it their way. I can advise and ask them to prove they are doing something to achieve an agreed goal, but as Covey said, 'You delegate results not methods'. I believe I have achieved this in my own business; I have a group of leaders who are self-motivated and want to achieve outcomes their way. At the same time, they cannot be completely dismissive and ignore my input. This is the point of the creative tension: for me to push, but equally to have a culture where they can push back. We need to be able to have robust and sometimes heated discussions to identify the best way to achieve something without a dominant ego insisting everything must be done its way. This is, of course, only possible with high levels of mutual trust.

The Alarm Bell plays a key role in this. As long as the result is delivered, I don't make too much of a fuss of how, unless it triggers my Alarm Bell.

Returning to the seasons metaphor – if the onset of winter is suspected or some genuine crisis has arrived and my Alarm Bell is ringing loudly, I will want to be more in Boss and find out what specifically my directors are doing. This is also part of their trust in me: if they agree this is a crisis, they now concede that my broader leadership perspective will be needed to help navigate out of stormy waters. However, that doesn't mean I become a dictator; I still want challenge from them – but once decisions are agreed, I expect them to fully and urgently engage with the resulting work.

During these winter periods, I also have often taken on wider management responsibilities. My Fox has to be especially alert at this time. I remember during a crisis having a one-on-one meeting with a relatively young team member, who, since the crisis began, had started to report directly to me. I knew that he had been very autonomous under his previous manager and although that worked well during autumn harvest, it wouldn't work now. My Fox knew he was very headstrong and needed to test if he would accept me as his leader. I said to him, 'I know that under your previous manager, you became the "power behind the throne" and I would like to thank you for your initiative'. My Coach noticed a half smile, showing that he appreciated the acknowledgement from my Compass. 'However', I went on, 'times have changed and that approach *won't work with me*'. I then gave him a firm look directly into his eyes and added, with grounded, yet intense Boss energy, 'Do you get what I am saying?' I was hoping he would nod and accept this call to accept my leadership. However, my Coach noticed his response: a contemptuous sneer along with the word 'Yes'. My Alarm Bell rang and my Boss knew at that moment that he would be unmanageable (and I therefore couldn't trust him). He would need to move on. I then went into Conductor, tactfully ending the meeting not letting on what I knew. I then could plan a controlled ending; no explosions or dramas needed.

Replacing people is, sadly, a key part of being a leader. Because my Coach has been more dominant than my Boss, looking back I could have avoided or mitigated many problems had I replaced underperforming people quicker.

One of the toughest and yet most necessary parts of leadership is knowing when someone can no longer cope with their role. Give them training and support, but at the end of the day when people are promoted beyond what they are able to do, keeping them there leads to dysfunctional people and a dysfunctional organisation. A successful business will grow, and sadly many of the people you work with will not grow at the same rate. Leadership is putting the needs of the business first. You can accommodate people to some degree, as no one is perfect, but keeping people in the wrong role ultimately becomes a lose-lose situation.

## Conclusion

I hope I have given a flavour in this chapter of how it is essential to become 'better than average' at each of these core functions to lead a team, to gain their respect and to understand the importance of these different and often competing perspectives. Only then can you work out if one of the players is 'out of tune' and help them play more harmoniously. Part of this process is to let your team evolve naturally, where they begin to manage and motivate each other without your presence. As my original coach, Ann Baldwin, said, 'Leaders will naturally fill a space – you can't push them into that space; they will either fill it or they won't'.

One of the key roles of leadership is to mentor other leaders. Each of your direct reports will be different, with specific biases due to them spending their career mainly within one function. Excellence is reached when each one of them – each section of the orchestra – will respect the others' (and your) judgement and collectively move forward, valuing these differences to produce great results.

Part of creating truly empowered function leaders is that they are not scared to make mistakes. The ability to learn from (rather than fear) mistakes is probably the most important part of the effective culture I mentioned above. The key is that mistakes are not hidden.

The ultimate leadership role is to help a new Conductor emerge within the business to 'play their music' without you being present – so you can then become the leader of a much larger group of companies, where all that is required is the occasional popping into to hear that music until winter arrives, when the orchestra will need to change its tune and some new players may be needed.

# Part III

# Mindfulness workbook

## Introduction

Welcome to the mindfulness workbook. The idea behind this section is that after trying a specific meditation practice, you can then design your own mindfulness course. There are a number of mindfulness apps and courses out there, and while they have good qualities, they can be very directional. The directions are presented as objective necessities, but often stem from the preferences of the person who designed the course. You may have different preferences: for example, some people's minds work along essentially visual lines; others – like me – are more auditory; others rely heavily on feelings. As you are a leader, I invite you to lead yourself into the best form of meditation for you.

I suggest you try this meditation once (if you have time) and then read the rest of the chapter. You can also listen to it (along with all the other practices in this section) at: www.nlpschool.com/meditate.

## The core meditation practice

1   Find a quiet place where you can sit and will not be disturbed for ten minutes.
2   Sit on a chair with your hands in your lap, your feet on the floor and your back relatively straight. You may wish to use a cushion to support your lower back.
3   Take a few moments to settle yourself. As your breathing slows, notice your heart beat and move your attention inward.
4   Focus on your body and move your awareness into your feet. Spend a few moments simply moving your awareness around your feet. Slowly move your attention upwards, noticing your ankles, shins, knees … Continue moving your attention slowly upwards so you become fully aware of different parts of your body. You don't need to do or change anything: just be aware of your body, of any areas of tension, or parts where you are relaxed. Be aware, perhaps, of some places you don't usually notice.
5   Now, notice the movements caused by your breathing. Allow yourself to breathe naturally. You don't need to change the pattern of breathing, just simply be aware of the subtle changes that occur in your body each time you breathe.

6   Start counting your breaths. Consider an inhale and exhale as a single breath. Count silently and softly to yourself. Breathe in, breathe out, count 'One'. Then in and out again, count 'Two' (and so on). After ten breaths, start again. Do this for about two minutes. If you lose the count, just start again at 'One'.

7   Count to yourself just before the *in*-breath. Count 'One', breathe in, breathe out. Repeat with 'Two', and so on, for the next two minutes. (This may seem similar to step 6, but when you try it, you will find it is quite different, as you will be anticipating the in-breath.)

8   For the next two minutes, stop counting and simply notice how the body breathes all by itself without interfering with this natural process. Notice the 'pulse' of the breath in different parts of your body. Can you sense this even in your fingers and your toes?

9   For the final two minutes, notice where the cool intake of breath hits your body first (the nose or throat usually) and where you feel the warmer out-breath. Focus on the physical sensations of the breath, including the temperature and movements of your body. Listen to the sound of the breath and other different sounds you make as you breathe – they may be different during different phases of breathing. Imagine breathing in different colours. Imagine that the colour darkens slightly as you breathe out; imagine toxins leaving your body. If you are able to do all three – feelings, sounds and images – simultaneously, this can be a particularly compelling way to quiet your inner thoughts.

10   Enjoy sitting in silence for a few more moments before slowly returning your attention to the room. Consider how your mood has shifted and set an intention for how you wish to conduct yourself before you continue your day.

Tip: Losing the count is quite normal. Every time it happens, don't worry about it, just gently and kindly return to the counting starting at 'One'.

Some people notice inner variations of this process: seeing images of the numbers for instance. This is fine, there are no 'rules' for how you experience your inner world. Just ensure you are able to practice this continuing process in a way that works for you.

## Meditation – tips, tricks and traps

### What are you looking to achieve?

At some level, the answer to this question is an oxymoron – the objective of meditation is literally to achieve nothing. However, I see it as a practice of finding a state where you are able to rest the mind's relentless search for outcomes. It is a sense of fascination with the present moment: you cannot be bored if you are fully absorbed in the huge array of sensations, pictures and sounds that you can experience in any moment.

The meditative state is not necessarily one of bliss but one of acceptance. 'This is how I am right now'. We often have a range of feelings playing out at the same time. To use a visual metaphor, we can become aware that there is an overall 'colour' of our mood in the present moment, perhaps dark, perhaps light – perhaps we aren't even exactly sure. At some level, it doesn't really matter for meditation practice, it simply is what it is – and by accepting what it is without wanting to change it, we notice (effectively benchmark) how we are right now. That is part of the symmetry of mindfulness: being able to be present and to switch into noticing that we are present (or not) so we can yet again return to being present. It is being able to hold whatever is there, in presence, without a need to change it. When we 'shine the light' of presence on ourselves, it is naturally and surprisingly transformative.

### What can go wrong?

To progress at meditation, you need to understand the various things that can distract you. Thoughts will attempt to take you away from the practice. When you notice this, remind yourself that you have chosen, for this period only, to take a 'time-out' from deliberately thinking, then gently bring yourself back to the practice. Notice the arising of these thoughts/feelings, but choose to let them go 'like clouds passing slowly across a blue sky' – you notice the cloud, but you choose not to engage with it and just return your focus to the meditation that you are doing.

However, this constant natural cycle of distraction and refocus can itself be a distraction – 'Why am I always distracted?' Accept that this cycle is what the practice is about; absolve yourself from feeling angry with yourself that you are unable to be permanently present.

Much of this distraction comes from what Eckhart Tolle, in his book *The Power of Now*, calls the ego, the competitive part of our mind that is absorbed by our own identity, and which is perpetually considering how that identity expressed itself in the past or will do so in the future. The ego doesn't like it when you are present. It feels abandoned and wants to plan ahead or recall the problems that motivate you to change. Although this motivation is a necessary part of us, we don't need so much of it. Spending so much time churning the same ideas over and over drains our energy so we find it harder to execute these very same plans. Also, although the future is important, when we arrive there it will be the present – so if we are unable to enjoy the present moment, the improved future that our ego is helping us build will be of little enjoyment or comfort to us when it finally arrives.

The ego also gets caught up in issues from our past, replaying narratives where people let us down and perhaps having revenge fantasies about how we will one day get even. The past can become a habitual place that we live in, satisfying the ego's need for emotional stimulation, even if that stimulation is negative. Our ego is fearful that meditation will lead us to abandon our future plans and past lessons – and thereby make it, the ego, redundant; no wonder it battles. However, once you practice meditation, the ego begins to realise that it is alive and well and not going anywhere. It might even enjoy a brief bit of respite.

We can also try too little or too hard. Stephen Gilligan quotes 1930s movie star and accomplished swordsman, Errol Flynn: 'Fighting with a sword is like holding a bird, if you hold the bird too tight – no bird [you kill it]. If you hold the bird too loose – no bird [it flies away]'. Not too loose and not too tight is the guiding principle. This is known in traditional meditation practice as 'appropriate effort'; too tight is 'excess effort' and too loose is 'lazy effort'.

Meditation involves gently balancing our effort level. Starting with appropriate effort, it can drift away into lazy effort; you then notice this and rush to fix it – excess effort – hoping to return to appropriate effort again. The quality of how you both notice these shifts and do something about them is also an important part of meditation practice. You kindly and lovingly notice that you have lost focus, and you then gently and kindly return to the practice. You don't do this like a detective finding and arresting a criminal, but like a horse whisperer – gently inviting a return. Mindfulness is a strange state where you are both highly attentive and highly relaxed.

There is science behind this human ability both to be engaged in something and to simultaneously be aware that you are engaged in it. Neurologist Wilder Penfield conducted experiments by stimulating the temporal lobe of awake patients who, through an unfortunate accident, had part of their brain exposed. These patients reported that the stimulation led them to re-experience specific memories depending where the probe was placed. One patient said, 'I not only remember how I felt, I feel the same way now'. This implies that this patient existed in two states simultaneously: he fully relived the past event, at the same time he was awake and interacting with Penfield and the other staff in the hospital (he was also about to go into surgery; Penfield didn't have long to do these experiments). The implications for meditation are profound – you can both feel present and notice how that presence is regularly interrupted by your thoughts. This neatly leads onto a classic way of categorising those interruptions: the Five Hindrances.

A key part of meditation is to learn how to hold uncomfortable feelings without having to enter a narrative about them. Just notice and accept whatever feelings you have, without pushing them away or attempting to engage with them. When you notice your thoughts have returned – pause and notice which of the following categories you can group those thoughts into:

1   Hatred or ill will (including feeling angry). Meditation is best avoided immediately after an angry encounter – it is best to cool off and wait a while. However, if you find that when you meditate, you frequently recall a mental shopping list of people or events that trigger your anger response, then this is useful information for you. It is a signal that you may benefit from dealing with these issues in a different way. However, from a meditation perspective it is best to simply be aware of those angry thoughts and then let them pass for now.

2   Desire for sensory experience (e.g. wanting to do something, wanting to think or fantasising). When I started meditating, I found it hard to be deprived of doing something even for a short time. Once I practiced a lot, I found much richness in simply enjoying the state of meditation – but it took time. I still find myself wanting to experience things when meditating:

I often start thinking about food or planning something nice to do. But when I notice I have started this pattern, I say to myself, 'I can plan later; for now, I will give myself this brief time to just meditate'.

3    Restlessness and anxiety (including trying too hard to meditate). This fits with 'excess effort': if you 'try harder' when you feel stressed, this can create a negative loop, where you increasingly try hard to feel relaxed and simply become more and more stressed. This can be an important lesson, that you actually need to move in the opposite direction (try less hard). Deliberately relaxing your body and moving your attention into your abdomen can remove these circular thoughts. Notice and acknowledge the pattern ('I'm feeling restless') and just gently return to the practice.

4    Sloth and torpor (including feeling sleepy or unmotivated). This fits with 'lazy effort'. Sometimes people are in a state of near permanent exhaustion and meditation can be a signal that they simply need to rest. However, if this happens frequently it can also be a tactic by your ego to avoid meditation, and you need to deliberately increase your energy level. Adjust your posture and sit up straight. You may also wish to try the walking meditation detailed later in the chapter.

5    Doubt and indecision (including being unsure of one's ability to meditate). Everyone has insecurities about learning and doing something new. Even highly experienced performers can suffer from 'freezing' and worry that they will lose their skills. This is also the ego's fear of becoming redundant, mentioned above, and partially a negative belief about your own abilities: 'I can't do this'. Name and acknowledge that sensation: 'I am feeling doubt and indecision and that is completely natural' and then return to the practice.

### Posture

Meditation is generally practised seated, either in a chair or on the floor.

On a chair, ensure that you sit upright, preferably near the edge of the seat, so your back isn't in contact with the back rest. If this is comfortable, sit back in the chair but stay upright. Put both feet firmly on the floor so your legs form a right angle at your knees (see diagram below).

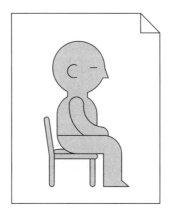

Once you are seated, do the following to get into the right posture. Sit upright so you are neither leaning forward or back, but instead feel the weight of your body in the middle of your 'sit bone'. Move your pelvis slightly forward and move your back so your shoulders are directly above your hips. Place your hands on your legs, palms up with your index finger and thumb lightly pinched, or just find a place where your hands and forearms can relax resting on your legs. Relax your shoulders and slowly nod back and forth until you find a position where your head feels like it is floating evenly on your neck. Imagine an invisible piece of string connected to the top back part of your head, pulling it up so your spine elongates and your chin tucks in slightly. Have a sense that your body is fully supported by the ground.

You can also sit on the edge of a cushion to help your pelvis move forward, and use another cushion to support your lower back.

On the floor, there are various postures. I would suggest starting by sitting on the edge of a pillow or yoga block with your legs crossed. This helps support your back and keeps your spine upright. Yoga was invented partially to relieve pains from long periods of seated meditation. Meditation shouldn't be painful, but if you find it is, then perhaps seek out a couple of beginners' yoga lessons (advanced ones can cause injuries for beginners). This can ensure you are sitting in the correct posture, and will also provide some useful stretching and mindfulness exercises.

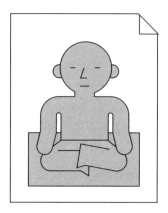

### *Entering and leaving a meditation practice*

Meditation has a slow and deliberate feel to it. Rushing in or out of it can defeat its purpose. After you have got into the correct posture, take a couple of minutes to sit quietly and allow your heart rate to slow and your body to relax.

Before I begin meditating, I often set a simple objective or intention, in the following form: 'I wonder if I can simply arrive in presence' or 'I wonder if I can do this process right now'. Sometimes I set an intention for some new way to appear to resolve a problem or stuck area in my life. Although this is not necessary, it is a good habit to sometimes consider what you hope to get out of a particular seated session. You can then let go of that intention during the practice and notice if something happened at the end of it.

Concluding the process is done in two phases. The first is not really an ending but the outcome of meditation – simply sitting in silence, not doing anything for a while but having a sense of inhabiting the present moment. This is where you are headed and as you become more experienced, you will want to spend as much of your meditation time in this silent state, using the various processes simply as vehicles to take you there.

Second, when you decide to end the practice, do this slowly. Start by gently moving your fingers and toes and slowly building a connection with the outside world before you open your eyes. Spend a few more moments sitting, noticing how you are, before you slowly get up and continue with everyday life.

## Design your own meditation course

Work out a place and a chair or mat where you will be able to practice on a regular basis – also where you will not be disturbed. Preferably, use this place from now on, and, if possible, at a similar time every day. I recommend doing this each morning soon after you wake up. If this is not practical in your situation, then commit to practice every day, whenever you can find the time. If you miss a day, don't give up: do your best.

Put in place some simple agreements with anyone you live with to minimise interruptions.

New practices require discipline to stick to a plan you effectively make with yourself. This will help you establish a habit. Give yourself slightly more than ten minutes, so you gain the habit of taking a pause before and after the practice. In the second week, if you can spare fifteen or twenty minutes, so much the better. Having a further practice before you go to bed is also recommended.

You may wish to simply continue for the next seven days with the core practice at the start of this chapter, or you can try different ones from the exercises suggested below.

I have put the exercises into four main types. The first type is breathing based (it features two meditations). The second concentrates more on the body and motion. The third features an exercise based around visualisation. A fourth section introduces two more complex meditations, which I suggest you leave until you have experience of the other meditations in this book.

I suggest you try an exercise from each of the first three sections, and find which works best for you. Once you have made this decision, work on this exercise for a week. This will 'raise your game' and enable you to work better with less familiar material. For the second week, try an exercise from a second category, and for the third week, from the remaining one.

However, as I've said, do it your way. Your inner world is yours. Part of the job of meditation is to help you realise that the rules of the outside world don't apply to your own imagination.

Please stop the practice (or pause briefly) if you become light-headed or start to feel unwell. Meditation should be relatively easy and most people don't have significant trouble with it. If you begin to hyperventilate or have a strong negative reaction, stop. If this continues, seek medical advice.

## 1 Breathing meditations

When stressed, our breath is also stressed – we restrict our breathing. Learning to deliberately release and to ease our breath relaxes us. This tension can also act as a signal that we need to shift into Conductor mode and become more disassociated. As breathing is one of the only bodily functions we can do both deliberately and unconsciously, the interplay between trying to watch our breath without interfering with it, and the natural urge to interfere with that which we are observing, makes meditation practices based on breathing common, effective and popular.

The lungs are not muscular. Breathing depends on the movement of the physical structures that support and surround them. You can roughly divide these into three sections: the ribs, the diaphragm and the shoulder girdle. This gives three distinct ways of breathing, which you can soon learn to notice in yourself and in others:

1   *Abdominal*, where the lungs are moved primarily by the diaphragm, which contracts downward while pushing the belly out. This causes inhalation, pulling air deep into the lower lungs. As the lungs are bell shaped, there is a larger area of alveoli (small sacs that oxygenate our blood) at the bottom of our lungs, therefore this form of breathing delivers more oxygen into your lungs per breath and oxygenates your blood more efficiently, which in turn can reduce your blood pressure, calming the body and thus the mind. It is desirable to spend some time deliberately breathing in this area. However, in our society people often want to have a small belly and can become preoccupied with keeping this area 'sucked in'. Deliberately relax your belly while you are meditating – no one is watching.

2   *Thoracic*, where the rib cage expands and contracts, moved by the intercostal (between the ribs) muscles. This pulls air into the centre of the lungs. Less oxygen than above is delivered to the blood per breath. However, this area is useful for rapid breathing, especially during exercise.

3   *Clavicular*, where the collarbone and shoulder bone and shoulder blades lift. This pulls air only into the smaller upper lobes of the lungs. This area has the least oxygenation effect, and breathing from it often causes tension in the neck and shoulders.

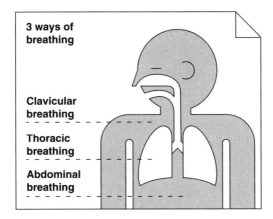

People tend to have habitual breathing patterns that emphasise one section over the others. Often these have a psychological basis. Someone who is frequently anxious will often habitually breathe in a clavicular manner, which in turn increases their level of stress. By contrast, deep abdominal breathing usually indicates calmness. When observing other people, you can learn a lot about their state by looking at their breathing (and related posture).

Take a little time to put attention on the section you use less: flexibility with your breathing is good for your health.

Tip: you can also 'pace and lead' from one type of breathing to another, especially to calm someone down. If they are stressed, they are likely to be breathing rapidly and 'high' (clavicular). Start there yourself, then slowly move your breathing, via the chest, to the lower, abdominal, calmer state. They should follow. Likewise, if you wish to energise someone, do the reverse.

The following exercises use breath, either changing the way you breathe physically, or simply directing the attention to the breath, or a combination of these.

### The 'Three Tyre' exercise

Start by noticing your breathing. What parts of your body move? What parts are touched by the expansion of air in your lungs? Get a sense of the internal effect of each breath.

Learning how to use each tyre:

1   Imagine there is a tyre round you just around the level of your navel.
2   As you breathe in, imagine this tyre expanding all around your lower abdominal region – your lower belly, sides and lower back. It may help if you imagine a white mist filling your belly as you breathe in and leaving when you breathe out.
3   As you breathe out, imagine this tyre contracting, by squeezing out the air around your lower belly, sides and lower back. Then stop the process and breathe normally without trying to change anything. Simply observe your breathing. How has it changed from before?

4   Now move the image of the tyre up around your ribcage, and expand and contract in the same way. Notice the expansion in the chest, shoulder blades, under your arms and sides of your ribs and upper belly. Then stop the process and breathe without trying to change anything. Again, simply observe your breathing and notice how it has changed from before.

5   Now move the image of the tyre up around the top of your shoulder and neck area, and expand and contract in the same way. Notice the expansion in your neck and shoulders. Then stop the process and breathe without trying to change anything. Simply observe your breathing. How has it changed from before?

The process:

1   Start at the lower tyre, around the belly button. Breathe in and 'inflate' the tyre. Then do the same with the ribcage (middle) tyre. Finally, imagine the top tyre around the top of your shoulders and inflate it.

2   To exhale, deflate the top tyre, the middle tyre and the lower tyre in that order.

3   You can continue inhaling and exhaling in this way continuously if that is comfortable. As you learn the process, it advisable to return to your normal breathing for a few breaths between each cycle before returning to the three-tyre breathing.

4   Return to normal breathing. Simply observe your breathing. Take a few minutes to simply sit in silence then come slowly back to the everyday world.

Tip: a simpler version of this is to use the lower, abdominal tyre on its own. A fast way I use to enter the Conductor is to have five deep breaths in the lower tyre. I can do this discreetly in a meeting.

### Moving the breath meditation

This is an extension of observing the breath and uses the concept of *dan tien*. In traditional Chinese medicine and martial arts, the body is seen as having three principal energy centres, or *dan tiens*. The process comes from Qi Gong, sometimes known as Chinese yoga, and focuses on the two lower *dan tiens* (i.e. the lower and middle tyres in the Three Tyre exercise). It draws attention to five qualities associated with breath in this tradition.

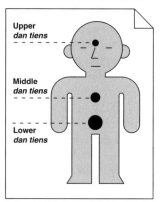

1 Begin by taking nine deep breaths, in through the nose and out through the mouth, filling the body with deep and full breaths.

2 Return to normal breathing through the nose. Imagine breathing into the middle *dan tien* (in the middle of your chest) and breathe out, letting the air drop down to the lower *dan tien* (in your lower abdomen, just below your navel). Repeat this nine times: breathe into your middle *dan tien* and imagine that, as you breathe out, the breath drops to your lower *dan tien*. If you wish, you can also imagine an image of white mist moving up and down as you do this.

3 The next cycle is the reverse: breathe into your lower abdomen, filling that area with breath, then breathe out, allowing the breath to move up to your middle *dan tien* as your belly deflates. Repeat nine times.

4 Now keep all breaths into and out of the lower *dan tien*. Breathe into your lower *dan tien*, feeling your lower abdomen, sides and lower back expand. Breathe out, imagining keeping the air within your lower abdomen, as if you were breathing internally. Have a sense of expansion and contraction, like an accordion. Feel it, and your sides and lower back, contract.

5 Repeat this for a time, then after each exhalation, in order to be aware of the five qualities of the breath, say to yourself: 'The breath is *long* (breathe in, breathe out), the breath is *deep* (breathe in, breathe out), the breath is *even* (breathe in, breathe out), the breath is *slow* (breathe in, breathe out), and the breath is *fine* (breathe in, breathe out)'.

6 Repeat this technique for as long as you wish, after a time stopping the words and just noticing a gentle 'pulse' of breath in and out of your lower *dan tien*. This is sometimes referred to as 'baby breathing'.
A variation of the above is to extend the time of these breaths in your lower *dan tien*. As you breathe in, count to five, pause, then count to five while you breathe out. Increase this count, while remaining comfortable. Meditation masters can inhale for 60 seconds and then exhale for 60, but this could take years to achieve. Another variation is to breathe in for a count of five; hold for a count of five; breathe out for a count of five; hold for a count of five (and repeat). Again, after a while increase the count. Some people like to visualise moving around the four sides of a square as they repeat this process.

Tip: you may like to imagine white (or some different colour) light moving between your chest and lower abdomen. During the last phase, you might like to imagine your lower *dan tien* glowing as you breathe in, then darkening as you breathe out. Perhaps imagine breathing out toxins with each exhalation. You may also focus on the different sounds of the breath in each section, as well as the sensations you feel as you breathe.

## 2 Body and movement meditations

### Body scan

This is a more detailed version of the starting section of the core practice.
Become comfortable in your seated posture and move your attention inwards.

As you breathe in, allow your attention to focus into the soles of your feet as they make contact with the ground. As you breathe out, allow your feet to relax. Continue breathing and noticing the soles of your feet in this way, for a few more breaths.

Repeat with your toes. Become aware of your toes. Breathe in, moving that awareness completely into your toes. As you breathe out, allow your toes to relax completely. Move your awareness around your feet: the spaces between your toes, the tops of your feet – visit all the areas of your feet with your 'mind's eye'.

Repeat this awareness as you move up to your ankles, calves, shins, knees, thighs, hips, pelvis, sacrum, lower back, middle back, spine, shoulders, neck, chest, arms, hands, fingers, belly, chest, face, eyes, cheeks, jaw, forehead – your entire body.

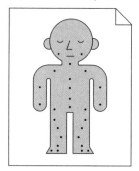

Allow this process to lead you to a sense of stillness, so you can again sit quietly in presence and stay like this for extended periods of time.

Tip: this can also be a good way to start other practices, deliberately relaxing your body before you begin, say, a breathing practice.

It can also be done lying down. Spend time noticing how your body makes contact with the ground or bed.

### Walking meditation

1    Allow yourself to stand and notice the numerous subtle movements you make to keep yourself standing. This took you about two years to accomplish. Be aware of all it takes, of the multitude of small adjustments you make each moment simply to be able to stand up.

Now, begin to walk at a slow but normal pace. Do all the following while on the move: don't stop to do any of them.

2   Notice the repeating pattern of lifting your foot through space and returning it to the ground. Notice how you roll across your foot as it first makes contact with the ground through your heel, then how that contact moves up to the ball of the foot and then across towards your toes. You then lift the other foot, which passes through the air until it too makes conract with the ground at its heel. Notice this repeat pattern of lifting and rolling across. Keep your awareness in your feet for a minute or so.

3   Now bring your attention to your ankles. Notice the subtle movements in your ankles as your foot moves in space and then meets the ground.

4   Repeat this by moving up your leg: calves, knees, thighs.

5   Be aware of your hips and allow them to relax as you walk. Notice that you can relax them even more and this may change the way you habitually walk. Keep relaxing your hips.

6   Now notice how your pelvis cuts out a three-dimensional shape in space as your hips move and your legs lift alternately. Try to visualise and feel this moving shape that your pelvis makes in space as you walk.

7   Now bring your attention to your spine. Your spine is connected to your sacrum (the large triangular bone that connects the spine to the pelvis) and as your pelvis moves, you will notice that your spine also moves in a subtle and bending way. Focus your attention on your spine as you walk and notice all of these subtle waves and bends as you move.

8   Now move your attention into your shoulders and allow your arms to swing naturally as you walk. Allow this swinging to gently massage your shoulders and neck as you walk. You may notice how your relaxed hips provide momentum to this process.

9   Now move your attention to your chest and belly, allowing them to relax.

10   Try lifting your head, up and down, so you slightly look up then slightly look down. Find a place somewhere in the middle to give you a nice balance of attention within (looking down) and outside (looking up). There is a position somewhere in the middle that balances your attention inward and outwards, which is like appropriate effort, aware of both the outside world and your inner thoughts and sensations at the same time.

11   Become aware of your breath and notice how many steps you naturally take per breath. Just become aware of this number, without needing to change it. Count both the number of steps per in-breaths and the number of steps per out-breaths.

12   Notice as much of the entire experience of your body as you can – see if you can combine all the sensations that have been detailed in the previous steps.

13   Allow yourself to just be present for a while.

14   Come to a stop. Take a few moments to reflect on your experience before continuing with your day.

## 3  Visualisation

### *Golden Light meditation*

For people who find it easy to think in pictures, this process has a more visual approach. If you find imagining pictures a struggle, it is still worth pretending to see pictures, even if this is a bit of stretch.

Perform the body scan (as described in Section 2 above): notice areas of comfort and discomfort.

1  Give yourself permission to be just as you are. You don't need to change anything; you don't need to do anything – just allow yourself to be how you are right now.
2  Take nine deep breaths: in through the nose, out through the mouth. Empty your mind, have no images.
3  Now, breathe in golden light. Fill your body with it.
4  Breathe out any toxins.
5  Take all further breaths through your nose. Do not force your breath; follow its natural rhythm.
6  Bring awareness to your spine.
7  Visualise a golden thread of light from your tailbone to the crown of your head.
8  Hold that image of a golden thread and continue breathing naturally. You may like to imagine that the thread sparkles. Notice the way it has been woven.
9  Increase the width of the golden thread to the width of a string of golden light and hold that image for a few moments. Allow the thread to extend further to the diameter of your little finger. Hold for a while then increase it to the width of your thumb. Hold for a while. Allow the expansion to continue.
10  Imagine sitting in a large cylinder of light, tailbone to crown.
11  Imagine letting that shape extend outside of the body so you see yourself sitting in a pillar of light which extends to cover your whole body.
12  Imagine the edges of that pillar gently and slowly turning into an egg shape, so you have and hold an image of yourself sitting surrounded in a large sphere (or golden egg) of light. Make that egg as large as you like, so you don't feel cramped inside it.
13  Allow the egg to shimmer from within, as if it is protecting and energising your body.
14  Hold that image for as long as you like.
15  Let the egg return to a pillar.
16  Let the pillar reduce and come into your body, running from tailbone to crown.
17  Then let it reduce to the width of your thumb, then to the width of your finger, then back to a thread.
18  Concentrate the thread into a point in your third eye (between your eyebrows). The entire energy of the egg is concentrated into one point of gold.

19  Imagine this dot of gold sinking in your body, down into your mouth. You swallow it and it goes down your throat into the lower abdomen, like the sun setting into an ocean of tranquillity.
20  As that image begins to fade, know that you can summon the power of the golden egg any time you need it.

Tip: if you find it hard to imagine images (as I do), just pretend you can do so. I bring my attention to the feeling in my spine and pretend I can 'see' the various threads. There is a sort of sixth sense called proprioception, our ability to notice our body in space. If you close your eyes, you can get a sense if you are upright or lying down; you have a sense of the space in front of you or behind you. By likewise sensing your spine, this ability can double up as a sort of 'half-feeling/half-seeing' way of experiencing this meditation.

Tip: I mentioned boundaries in the section on Yin archetypes above. I also use the imagery from this meditation if I feel threatened by someone whom I feel has a negative intent towards me. I simply imagine a sort of 'shield' between us, that anything this person may say or do will simply 'bounce off' my shield. I am not suggesting this can be used in a violent confrontation – it is more of psychic shield. It may seem a bit weird, but it works.

I should also mention that there are meditations for people whose preference is auditory. Meditators can direct their attention to a sound made internally. This sound is called a mantra: 'Om' is the classic one. Just repeat this sound silently (or out loud) as a meditation practice. The commercially successful transcendental meditation falls into this, auditory category.

For a meditation that involves more than one way of taking in and processing information, try focusing simultaneously on what you see, hear and feel at the same time. I can look at a tree, hear the wind (or other sounds around me) and feel the wind (or other sensations) on my body. Notice how you tend to spend more time with one of these senses than others. Notice how your mind 'pauses' on one sense and you can practice staying with all three.

## 4  Advanced meditations

I recommend that you do not try these unless you are an experienced meditator or you have practiced the preceding material on a regular basis for at least six months. The first of these I practice rarely, perhaps every six months – the second you can practice any time (but please try the first one first).

### 'Life Purpose' meditation

This is something that I would practice every six months or so. It was originally created for workshops I led with Edward Hines. I have since taught it for over fifteen years with remarkable results.

This meditation will invite you to consider how your values and goals might change if you knew that you only had a finite and specific amount of time left to live. For this to work effectively, and not just upset you, it is important that you believe you are in perfect health throughout the process. Even if you are not now, imagine that you are for the purpose of this meditation. Imaging that you will become ill or suffer will be an unhelpful (and unkind) distraction. Also, try to remain detached – in Conductor mode. The purpose of the process is to discover what is truly important to you, not to torture yourself. Therefore, if you start having negative thoughts or images, detach yourself by imagining that you can see yourself going through this process, while the 'you' watching just learns anything useful without getting overwhelmed. Teaching this practice, I have found that older people sometimes worry about the ten years being a literal end of their lives. This isn't helpful. The meditation is an imaginative practice (you are making it up), and it is best to simply believe you will be alive and well after ten years. The practice itself usually brings great benefits, inspiring unexpected and pleasing new attitudes.

1   Settle yourself for a few minutes. When you are ready, point to the future. Just do this without thinking. Note the direction in which you sense the future will be.

2   Move along an imaginary line in the 'future' direction you discovered above, to an imagined point in that future. At this point you have exactly ten healthy years left to live. Ask yourself 'What do I want to accomplish?' and 'What is important to me now?'

3   Move along that same line nine more years, to where you will have exactly 12 healthy months left to live. Ask yourself, 'What do I want to accomplish?' and 'What is important to me now?'

4   Move along the line 11 months, to where you will have exactly four weeks left to live. Ask yourself, 'What do I want to accomplish?' and 'What is important to me now?'

5   Move along that line three more weeks, to where you will have exactly seven days left to live. Ask yourself, 'What do I want to accomplish?' and 'What is important to me now?'

6   Move along that line six more days, to where you will have exactly 24 hours left to live. Ask yourself, 'What do I want to accomplish?' and 'What is important to me now?'

7   Move along that line 23 more hours, to where you will have exactly 60 minutes left to live. Ask yourself, 'What do I want to accomplish?' and 'What is important to me now?'

8   Move along that line 59 more minutes, to where you will have exactly 60 seconds left to live. Ask yourself, 'What do I want to accomplish?' and 'What is important to me now?'

9   This last section you can repeat a few times – no rush, try it out:

10  Move along that line to a point in the future, when you will take your last breath – breathe in and ask yourself, 'What do I want to accomplish?' and 'What is important to me now?'

Tip: you may wish to practice or repeat the last step a few times. This exercise is simply a thought experiment, so vary it to make it easy for you.

Hyrum Smith said that the purpose of life is the acquisition and maintenance of inner peace. I hope as you practice this meditation, what is truly important to *you* comes into focus and what is beyond your control you can learn to accept in peace.

Death is the natural existential fear and a subject rarely discussed. Historically, death would have been far more visible, but it is largely hidden in our society. By contrast, the book *Staring at the Sun* by psychologist Irvin Yalom describes people for whom an encounter with death has been an 'awakening experience', which truly transformed their lives. Modern psychology tends to assume that human problems come from past experiences, but failure to deal with existential, forward-looking questions of purpose and mortality can be destructive too. As Nietzsche said, 'He who has a why to live for can bear almost any how'.

### Five aggregates meditation

This process can be practiced at any time. The principle behind it is that our ego will cling on and refuse to let us detach at each stage of the meditation. The process starts with the body, then moves to feelings, then thoughts, then mental functioning and finally consciousness, which is an aggregation of the first four. After each phase, imagine a place you can 'sit in' and observe yourself – I call this the space of the silent watcher – and observe yourself having just let go of that part of your conscious awareness. I imagine this watcher located behind me to my upper right; you may find creating a specific place to locate your silent watcher helpful too. For all intents and purposes, this silent watcher is your Conductor.

### 1 Body

Become aware of your body and the energy in your body. Pay attention to different parts of your body in turn, and become aware of the physical sensations within them. You don't need to interpret them (for example as emotions); just allow yourself to notice them.

You can also expand this awareness internally to your organs, including those that enable your senses (eyes, ears etc.), and the incredible way these function within you. Say to yourself, 'I have a body and my body is amazing; at the same time, (pause) I am more than just my body'. Allow yourself to let go of an attachment to physical sensations arising within the body. Sit and observe yourself from the position of the silent watcher for a while and then move on to the next phase.

### 2 Feelings

Now bring your attention to your feelings and emotions. Begin simply by noticing them and acknowledging their existence. Bring your awareness to your emotions within your body and allow yourself to truly appreciate these emotions. Say to yourself, 'I have emotions, and my emotions are amazing; at the same time, (pause) I am more than my emotions'. Allow yourself to let go of an attachment to these emotions (and related sensations arising within the body) for a little while.

### 3  Thoughts and perceptions

Now bring your attention to that part of your body where thought arises – often this is within the forehead area. Allow yourself to notice the sensation of thinking as an actual event in your head, rather than engage with the thoughts. You will begin to notice the arising of thoughts, fantasies and perceptions. Allow these to exist and acknowledge them without engaging in them – just appreciate them. Again, say to yourself, 'I have thoughts, and my thoughts are amazing; at the same time, (pause) I am more than my thoughts'. Allow yourself to let go of an attachment to thinking and the associated sensations associated with this. Sit and observe yourself from the position of the silent watcher.

### 4  Mental functions

Now bring your awareness to that part of your mental processing that is not done in the neocortex in your forehead, (the part which does the 'human thinking'). Such work is done in other parts of your brain, your spinal column and processing centres around your heart and belly. Allowing awareness to move everywhere inside these areas, especially your head, separating out the section you previously attributed to thoughts. This part of your body may not be a familiar place to direct attention, but it is likely that much of your unconscious mind and control functions reside within these areas.

Simply allow your awareness into this area and become aware of the power that exists within it. If you start becoming overwhelmed, return your attention just behind your head. Go to the silent watcher position, so that you can imagine the 'you' behind yourself becoming aware of the sensation within that area of your body. Say to yourself, 'I have mental functions and my mental functioning is amazing and at the same time, (pause) I am more than my mental functioning'. Allow yourself to let go of an attachment to these sensations arising within that area of the body. Sit and observe yourself from the position of the silent watcher for a while.

### 5  Consciousness

Now allow yourself to know that you are conscious. A way of experiencing consciousness is to combine the previous four states into a new fifth state. First, revisit the physical sensations of the body. Now add the sensations of emotions within the body, combining the two states. Now become aware of the 'thoughts and perceptions' part of the body, combining it with the previous two. Now become aware of the 'mental functioning' part of the body, combining it to the previous three. Notice how these four states combine into a fifth state: your consciousness.

Say to yourself, 'I have consciousness and at the same time, (pause) I am more than just my consciousness'. Allow yourself to let go of an attachment to consciousness. As you again return to the silent watcher, this time allow yourself to be the observer of your consciousness. This silent part of you remains present at all times, yet often in the din of consciousness, your awareness of it is somehow distracted. Yet you can know that this part is ever present, watching in a state of acceptance and benevolence. You can know that this is part of you, and you can allow yourself to fully experience its beauty, depth and power.

Apart from www.nlpschool.com/meditate I have found listening to meditation MP3s of Ken Cohen (www.qigonghealing.com) and Bodhipaksa (www.bodhipaksa.com) very helpful. There are also various apps which also include different recordings of meditations packaged in a graphically pleasing way.

# Part IV

# Mission and vision workbook

This section deals with the creation of your own personal mission statement and vision metaphor. The mission statement is crafted from a few words and the vision metaphor is a mental image, sound or feeling. I cover two ways of doing this (once you have covered the values hierarchy and roles exercises below):

1   Where the values and roles naturally lead you to create a mission statement and vision metaphor.

or

2   A longer NLP style process to help you create the statement and metaphor

I would suggest you take some time to do this work. It can all be done in a couple of hours, but I recommend giving yourself a proper break to complete this. If you are pressed for time, you can do each section separately.

## Values hierarchy

Decide which are your top ten values, then write brief explanations of what they mean to you. These explanations don't need to be long or convoluted. A couple of sentences will do. For example, one of my values (as I hope this book has shown) is trust, and my explanation of it is 'Maintain intent without taking control. Let things unfold in their own way'.

Here is a list of potential values:

| | | | |
|---|---|---|---|
| Achievement | Equality | Legacy | Relaxation |
| Adventure | Excitement | Love | Reliability |
| Beauty | Exercise | Loyalty | Respect |
| Certainty | Faithfulness | Meritocracy | Responsibility |
| Charm | Freedom | Moderation | Sexuality |
| Cleanliness | Fun | Money | Significance |
| Communication | Health | Optimism | Sophistication |
| Connection | Honesty | Organisation | Strength |
| Conservation | Humility | Peace | Tolerance |
| Consideration | Industry | Physicality | Tranquillity |
| Contribution | Integrity | Pleasure | Variety |

| Courage | Intelligence | Politeness | Vision |
|---|---|---|---|
| Creativity | Intimacy | Power | Warmth |
| Dependability | Justice | Presence | Wealth |
| Discipline | Kindness | Progress | Well-being |
| Duty | Learning | Purpose | Wisdom |

Now *rank* your chosen values in order of importance to you. Once you have listed them and written a brief description of what they mean to you, write each one on a post-it note (or bit of paper) and put them in order of importance. Do this until you are happy with the order, then check it by asking yourself: 'If I had to get rid of one of these values, which would it be?'

Continue doing this until there is only one left. Then double-check by asking yourself: 'If I could recover *one* of the removed values, which would I choose?' Repeat this until ten are back on the table. The order is often not the one that you first thought it was. Make sure your values are ranked according to how you actually feel about them, not how you 'should' feel about them.

## Roles

This has a similar structure to the values exercise.

People play various roles in life. The purpose of this exercise is to take a Conductor view of all the roles you play (or want to play). This can help you detach from the role you perform at work and see your life in a wider context.

This process can be surprisingly powerful and transformative. A student on one of my courses didn't list the role of 'partner' although she had been married to the same man for over 20 years. She told me that she had realised during this exercise that although she was married, she and her husband had stopped playing a relationship role many years ago. This realisation transformed their relationship.

Make a list of your roles. You can have any number in any category.

1    Work roles, such as manager, coach, leader, salesperson, accountant, IT specialist, engineer, artist, negotiator, designer.
2    Non–work roles, such as parent, daughter, son, sibling, uncle, aunt, cousin, friend, neighbour, colleague, lover, partner, husband, wife, community, hobby, homeowner.
3    Roles you would like to play, but may need to wait until you are older or until current responsibilities diminish, such as charity, politics, investor, traveller, explorer, writer, artist, musician, sports person, community, religious.
4    Roles you could consider stopping playing. Roles are a choice; are there any you would like to stop now or would consider stopping after a while?
5    Roles you have stopped playing that you would benefit from playing again. These include relationships, both personal and business. We often see relationships as outcomes, but they are actually a continuing, dynamic role. You need to work at relationships for them to be a success. You may also at times need to instigate new relationships, especially in business. An

example could be to spend some time with customers to find out 'from the horse's mouth' how your business is delivering.

6    Your four well-being roles. We all need to incorporate roles to maintain our well-being. Often people miss out one or more of the following: *health* (diet, exercise, rest), *mental* (reading, courses, learning, etc.), *emotional* (relationship and social) and *spiritual* (meditating, time in nature, praying). A suggestion by Stephen Covey is that you need to spend at least one hour a day equally spread on the above activities (say two hours a week on each). A practical tip can be to combine them – take exercise or attend a course with a friend for instance. Overall, they will keep you sharp, balanced and happy. This is an essential part of leadership: exhausted and miserable leaders do not inspire. Gandhi's famous comment 'Be the change you wish to see in the world' applies here: as a leader, you need to embody the success you wish to create.

Put your roles in order of importance. You may wish to set some goals for some of the important roles you have neglected.

Armed with an understanding of your values and your roles, and the relative importance you attach to all of them, you can then go on to craft a mission statement and vision metaphor.

## Mission statement and vision metaphor

This section deals with a way of summarising these values and roles into words and then into something more visceral.

This is about putting yourself into a state where you feel a sense of alignment to your life purpose – the direction of your life. I want to help you create a kind of miniature ritual that enables you to enter into this state. I have found that although words work for some people, others prefer an image or a sound, or even prefer to feel a certain sensation in their body. This can be extended to smells and tastes – if a certain perfume or taste works, then why not use it? The belief that a brief statement of words is the only way to bring about this state is simply wrong – for some people, recalling an image of say, a waterfall, may be the way to bring this about.

I have found that a *combination* provides the best way to do this. It might be a verbal mission statement plus a visual image or specific sound, which is the vision metaphor. For me, the statement is 'Loving freedom will change the world – open sesame'. The metaphor is the Beatles song 'All you need is love'. (I have what is called in NLP an 'auditory' preference.)

This mission statement deals with both ways and means. By loving freedom (my values of both love and freedom), the world (and me, as I am part of that world) will change and evolve, and the treasures (in the widest sense of the word) of the Aladdin story – a young boy from an ordinary background who discovered things of huge value – will become available to me.

I also believe a mission needs to express both your personal ambition (to find Aladdin's treasure) as well as your higher purpose, to be of service to something greater than yourself (to change the world).

I also suggest that you keep the statement short – mine is seven words – so it is easy to remember.

You may find that through the process of identifying your roles and values, your mission statement and vision metaphor just 'appear' to you (as I described under the Compass section during my retreat in France). I believe that your mission is already something within you. You don't invent it – you put yourself into the right state to discover it. You may already have a strong sense of what it is.

I have, however, provided a more structured NLP exercise that I have found a very powerful way to help this discovery process.

### Timeline vision process

This is a helpful exercise for creating a strong mission statement and vision metaphor. It uses the NLP process of creating a timeline of your own life – past, present and future.

### Part one

Review your values and roles before you begin this exercise.

Use the timeline you discovered in the first step of the life purpose meditation (or read the section so you can have a sense of where you perceive your future to lie spatially).

Gesture to create a timeline on the floor in front of you that fits comfortably into the space you are in – as a rough guide the line is typically two to four times your height. It is an imaginary line that represents the majority of your life. It is best to think of it from birth to some future date when you will be 'older, healthy and wise'.

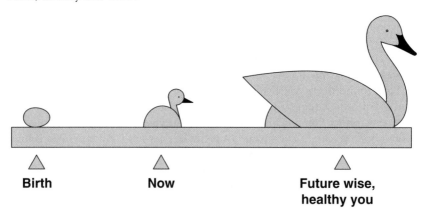

|  |  |  |
|---|---|---|
| **Birth** | **Now** | **Future wise, healthy you** |

Stand somewhere in the middle of the line, in a place that represents the present to you, then step off the line so you are standing in front of that position and you can survey the entire line.

Think of one of your first positive memories. Point to where it is on the timeline.

Think of certain key, positive events in your life such as your first day at school, your first day at work, the first time you tried a food you like, and point to where each of these are on the timeline. If any of these have unpleasant associations, then choose something else. This is called calibrating the line and it is best done by choosing memorable and pleasant events. I suggest you pick three.

Now think of a future date you have planned and are looking forward to, such as a holiday or time with friends and family, and point to where this is on the timeline.

Imagine a future goal you would like to achieve, and point to where that is on the timeline.

## Part two

Staying off the line, walk back beside it until you are next to one of the early past events.

Step onto the line and fully experience that event again. Allow yourself to become a child: move in that way again as if you were back there now. Allow yourself to fully relive that childhood moment and really enjoy it.

Once you have truly re-experienced those feelings and the memory, step back off the line.

Repeat with the two next experiences you picked from your past.

Now walk to the future pleasant event you picked and likewise step onto the line. Use your imagination to build a short narrative and imagine having a great time.

Step off and move to a point in the future, just after you achieve the goal you set yourself. Move slightly forward and imagine how that goal has already changed your life.

## Part three

Walk to the present and step onto the line.

Face the future and walk to a future point where you are older, healthy and wise.

Notice what life is like for you at this point.

You may wish to notice if any words or a metaphor, symbol, sound come to mind to represent this positive future. (You can use this to help craft your mission statement and the vision metaphor). Don't worry if nothing appears, just continue with the process.

Turn around, face the younger you on the timeline and offer them some advice. You may want to give them a metaphoric 'gift' and somehow send this down the timeline.

Stepping off the timeline, walk back beside it until you reach the present, then stand on the line again.

Look to the future and receive the message from the future you.

Note how you feel and what you think, hear and see. Make notes. This will help you build your personal mission statement and vision metaphor.

Read your roles and values again – try and craft some words that work for you.

Tip: Write down your statement along with the vision metaphor, roles and values somewhere you can easily refer to. I have mine stored on my computer's desktop. Make sure you keep it somewhere you can easily get to it and won't lose it. You may wish to include a photo or mp3 of a sound or song.

Tip: Create your own ritual. Find a time each week when you can re-read the statement, envisage your vision metaphor and review your roles and values. The intention is to return you to a state when you received the advice from the 'future you'. (I would do this before you start making plans for your forthcoming week. This helps you align your activities with what is truly important to you.)

Tip: People often have a vision metaphor from nature, but there are no rules – just pick something that reconnects you to the feelings you received from the 'future you'. This could be an image, a sound, a warm feeling – literally anything that works for you. If you are finding nothing comes up, go for a brief walk and pick something at random from your environment that feels good, such as a tree or building. Run with this as a vision metaphor. You can always replace it if something comes up later.

Tip: Take time to craft your mission statement. It is fine if it is a bit rambling to begin with. I found the process of refinement took a long time, with regular revisits. My mission statement of 'Loving freedom will change the world – open sesame' came to me a couple of years after my visit in France; my original mission statement seemed more like a mission essay! On the other hand, beware of the Tinkerer here. Don't change it every day: let it evolve, but at a certain point you will have found it and then you have it. Remember, its purpose is to reconnect you to the original state.

I have a mission meditation, which I recorded at www.nlpschool.com/meditate.

# Part V
# Appendices

# Appendix A: beliefs that hold you back

Some of the beliefs in this section may not apply directly to you. I have found, however, that they are commonly held. I suggest you read them anyway, to appreciate how other people can be held back by their beliefs.

## Beliefs about technical skills

As I have said, leaders need to adopt a specific approach to managing specialists. I hope I have already made clear the dangers of leaving technical or professional decisions to experts. The 'better than average' motto really has leverage here. Yet many leaders fail to do this. Why?

One reason is that some people think that technical matters are 'too complicated' to understand fully, so decisions in these areas have, regrettably, to be left to the experts. Examples of such areas are finance, law, marketing, production, design, human resources (HR) and information technology (IT).

Fear of finance can be rooted in difficulties at school with maths: 'I can't do long division'. Fear of law can be rooted in difficulties with English: 'I can't understand Shakespeare'. Poor teaching or unhelpful parental comments can sow the seeds of deep self-doubt in these subjects. This negative belief can then be encouraged by professionals: 'Leave it to me'.

Negative beliefs about one's competence with technical issues are best changed to 'I *can* understand this material and I will keep asking questions until I do.'

Another unhelpful belief is that technical skills are boring, and that leaders have better, grander, more leader-like things to do. This can be fuelled in organisations by years of hearing cynical or defensive comments about other departments. Leaders need to stand above petty interdepartmental rivalries and equally embrace all disciplines. The Conductor must not favour any instrument (especially their own); the focus is on harmonising these different and sometimes opposing forces.

Linked to such prejudice is the personal experience of not enjoying working in these areas. Don't confuse not liking something with not being able to do it. Remember that you don't have to love these activities, just respect them and be *good enough* at them.

The key point is that leaders don't actually 'do' these activities, they just need to understand them sufficiently to manage and, when necessary, challenge the expert.

## General beliefs about work

As children, we are encouraged to work. We are told to do our homework, clean our room or do household chores. We see our parents and relatives working and are commonly told, 'Be a good boy/girl and work hard'. Parents want to teach their children to become self-sufficient so they will be able to do well when their parents are no longer able to provide for them.

However, this culture of work has deeper social roots. Class systems define people's role in society by their work. In many traditional societies, aristocrats did not work – the English term 'gentleman' implies that the person didn't get involved in trade, but did more 'gentle' pursuits such as hunting, writing and painting. Work was for the lower classes. The very term working class implies that to be part of that clan, you need to work.

The rules of traditional societies were viciously enforced. I highly recommend the book *Discipline and Punish* by the French writer, Michael Foucault, or *The Angels of our Better Nature* by Stephen Pinker. Even as late as the early 1800s, the death penalty in Britain and France was still conducted as a long sadistic and public ritual. People were burnt at the stake in Germany in the nineteenth century (20,000 people gathered to watch arsonist Johannes Thomas die this way in Eisenach in 1804).

One could argue that the basic history of all societies is that some warlord with a band of thugs gained control of an area of land and eventually a monarchy and army were created. If members of that army refused to fight, they were treated so badly that other members were terrified and obeyed orders. The practice of keelhauling, for example, involved dragging sailors under a boat so they would be cut up by barnacles: they rarely survived. The British Navy didn't formally end this practice this until 1720. Foucault observes that post-revolutionary France was entirely structured along the Napoleonic military system: prisons, government, hospitals, schools and even businesses were organised like the army. Pinker says that Napoleon effectively turned the country back into a fascist monarchy.

The reason for this dark detour into our (fairly recent) past is that society hasn't changed as much as we might imagine. It is important for the leader to understand why people feel compelled to 'work' and therefore why so many people have trouble working efficiently or delegating. They fear that their work might end. Historically, work was something in service of the king, and failure to work for the king meant a painful death. The culture of the 'king' has expanded into our offices, schools and factories where a command to work is loudly trumpeted, even though there is no true king left (or even any memory why we had to do this work for a long-forgotten tyrant). I really do believe that lurking in our collective psyche is old programming that if we don't work we will be tortured to death, just as the original workers were in the army. This may seem ridiculous, but isn't the office simply a modern version of the army, with the directors playing the role of generals?

## Beliefs about 'your place' and identity

The other main purpose of these cruel punishments was to keep people in their place. The last thing any king wants is a revolt, or even someone grabbing too much power for themselves – Henry VIII disposed of men like Thomas Cromwell and Cardinal Wolsey who built their own power bases too successfully. People are socially programmed to follow and obey the king. They feel fear at the prospect of leading, because of stories of rise and fall where the fall is vicious and humiliating.

I see this fear of challenging 'knowing your place' in the modern business environment playing out all the time. I have a sad story about a man who was given the opportunity to become a regional CEO of a large global multinational; I will call him Sean. When he was promoted to become a director, his company hired me to be an executive coach for him. Sean was a highly intelligent and experienced professional, but had never held the position of director before. He valued hard work and prided himself on his ability to put in long hours and never took time off sick. He came from a humble background and was highly self-motivated and educated. However, he found it hard to delegate; often his emails would build up to such an extent that he began to hide them in an elaborate system of subfolders. During a frank and open discussion, I asked Sean how he would feel if he came to work and found his inbox empty – at that point, Sean took in an intense breath and with wide eyes blurted out, 'I would be useless'.

I advised Sean that his response was 'an identity level issue' and asked if he would be willing to do some deeper NLP work around identity. Sean agreed. He was intelligent and introspective and seemed to want to get to the bottom of this. We had several further sessions but I got the sense that at a deep level, Sean didn't really want to change: during a moment of quiet reflection he suddenly let out, 'I pulled myself up by my bootstraps and nothing is going to send me back down – I hate people who don't work hard and I will not become one of them!' A few months later Sean suddenly stopped replying to emails. He left the company shortly afterwards. I was very sad about this, as I liked him and knew that in many ways he wanted to succeed as a leader.

Sean never overcame his need to work in his original role. His past success had been built on it. But to lead, he had to find someone with the appropriate skills to replace his old role, so he could move on and become the Conductor. The reality of leadership is that you can't fully learn to lead until you start in the job. If you hobble yourself by becoming embroiled in your old role, you won't give yourself the necessary time to learn how to lead the other functions, by actually 'doing' leadership.

Leadership is not for everyone: it requires a huge effort to overcome a lot of programming from our youth. Work hard! Don't stand out! Above all, perhaps: who do you think you are?

When someone introduces themselves, they often say, 'I am an x' (x could be actor, accountant, nurse, teacher, builder, etc.). Ultimately, they have identified with a skill that they have mastered. This is common; our role in society is often governed by what we do. Achieving mastery of a skill is indeed a good accomplishment. However, from a leadership perspective, if you identify with a work role, you prevent yourself from transcending that role into leadership.

Identity is a powerful force. It is formed in infanthood, during separation from our mother (or original caregiver). This separation can be deeply traumatic: at some point, the infant becomes aware that they are separate from their mother, and, thus, alone and in terrible danger. Our first sense of independent identity can be a 'second birth' of dread and a deep fear of death. This is why identity is such a fragile construction: when someone is rejected socially or builds a sense of self on a job role which they then lose, these feelings can be deeply woven into that original sense of abandonment. The unconscious may believe that giving up a job role is equivalent to that same terror we experienced in early childhood.

In later childhood, as mentioned above, our parents will say some variation of 'Be a good boy/girl and work hard'. We can then believe that we are only worthy for what we do rather than who we are. This association is very common in people and adds to the work compulsion mentioned above. Identity becomes enmeshed with doing. We are told we don't have permission to simply be – to exist we have to *do*. This is why mindfulness can be so challenging.

Understanding the power and the illusion that is identity is an essential part of transitioning into leadership. There are many beliefs to overcome in order to shift identity: the social standing of 'a good job', the social conditioning to protect us from being keelhauled and to know our place. The transition to a leadership identity is a truly philosophical journey, not just a practical one.

# Appendix B: psychology

## TA, NLP and the NLP Matrix Coach

### Transactional Analysis

I have found the following material particularly useful for the Coach archetype. It provides an easy to understand model of the human psyche, which I find invaluable in business. It is also a direct and practical way of understanding shadows.

Transactional Analysis (TA) was developed by Eric Berne, a Freudian-trained psychiatrist, in the 1950s and 1960s. He was a brilliant observer of human interactions, with an eye for patterns of behaviour, which he then turned into elegant, powerful and user-friendly models.

In this section, I shall look at his basic PAC model. Berne postulated that people operate in three modes or 'ego-states', that of Parent, Adult and Child. (In this section, I shall use the capitalised word to mean the inner ego-state, and the uncapitalised one to mean an actual person: someone's parent or how they were as a child.)

Unlike many psychological concepts, these ones are refreshingly like what we expect them to be from their names. When we are in Parent, we are re-running behaviours, beliefs, values and even identities which we took on uncritically from our parents (and other authority figures from childhood). These can appear as beliefs such as 'people should be fair, just and kind'. When people are not, we can become very upset because of this 'rule' we uncon-sciously took on from our parents when we were young. A more helpful belief would be that, sadly, people are not always fair, just or kind, so when they are not, we can accept it more easily. In Child, we similarly revert to those beliefs that we developed or practised as children. Child beliefs are likely to create unhappiness by causing rebellion against the inner Parent: 'I don't want to restrain myself, I want to have fun'. In Adult we are rational, present and in control of ourselves, competent and not acting out archaic patterns from our past. The Adult can help notice and rephrase unhelpful Parent beliefs. It can also act as a mediator between Parent and Child, agreeing to allow the Child some 'fun' without binging and excess.

Both Parent and Child ego-states have positive and negative manifesta-tions. The legacy from our parents has a lot of useful material about things like looking after ourselves and behaving ethically. TA calls this the 'Nurturing Parent'. But there are also a whole lot of 'oughts' and 'shoulds', which can be oppressive if we do not examine them rationally (i.e. as adults) and either reject or accept them. TA calls these the 'Controlling Parent'. That critical voice we hear in our mind saying something like, 'Give up or you will just be disappointed' is an example of the Controlling Parent. Freud's term 'Superego' is effectively the Controlling Parent, and Freud's 'Ego' is the Adult.

Our retained Child similarly has helpful and unhelpful sides, reflected in the two words 'childish' and 'childlike'. The childish self – overly compliant or sulky and rebellious – is called the 'Adapted Child'. The creative, fun, and spontaneous (childlike) side is called 'Natural Child'. Berne introduced the concept of the Child, which is missing from Freud's three-part model, which instead talked about the Id, which he saw as a kind of primal essence and drive.

When managing people, it is easy to slip into the shadow of Controlling Parent (the Bully or Steamroller). This can send the recipient into Adapted Child (Headless Chicken, Creep or Crook), when they will either panic, become directly bolshie or passive-aggressive (outwardly compliant but planning revenge inside). Clearly, problems are best addressed and people best dealt with from the rational Adult position – be honest; don't score 'points'; see the other person's point of view.

One of the common patterns I have noticed in coaching executives is the 80:20 rule – they often spend 80 per cent of their management time on 20 per cent of their staff who are underperforming and troublesome. This is obviously wrong: staff that are performing well also need support and mentoring. Dysfunctional staff often have a concealed motivation, to get attention. As long as you continue in your role as a Controlling Parent, they will not change as they are getting the thing they have sought. This pattern is best explained by the following model.

### The Drama Triangle

Turn on the television, open a newspaper or listen to that particular friend who always seems to be complaining, and you will soon see the Drama Triangle in action. People are described as being on the triangle if they are acting out one of three roles: Persecutor, Rescuer or Victim.

Drama occurs when you move along the Triangle, moving from one of these positions to another.

Here is a simple example. A direct report sends in an important document late, along with an email containing excuses. This is something that has occurred before and you feel angry. You meet with this report to express your disappointment and that you expect work to be completed by the deadline, but you slip over into Bully. The person now becomes very upset and apologetic and explains that they had a genuine personal emergency. (In fact, they did not: you have been tricked by their Creep.) You begin to feel guilty, and rather than stay in Boss, you change into Psychoanalyst mode. During your advice giving you notice a devious half-smile and sense their Crook. Afterwards you feel aggravated and perturbed.

What has happened here is classic Drama Triangle. You started well, but as you slipped into Persecutor (Bully) they responded by becoming Victim (Creep). You then switched roles to Rescuer (Psychoanalyst) and they now feel victorious: they have turned the tables on you and you have become the Victim while they have become the Persecutor (Crook). In this example, you would have been better to have stayed in Boss and concluded with clear consequences if future deadlines are not achieved.

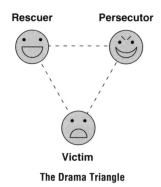

**The Drama Triangle**

If you find yourself in one of these Triangles:

- Go to Conductor. This is your Adult. Decide which archetype is appropriate for the situation, and don't get hooked into responding inappropriately.
- Bring the encounter to a speedy but professional conclusion.
- Be honest with yourself. Are you secretly getting some kind of psychological payoff from this, too?

Modern business needs to be conducted efficiently, and that means Adult to Adult. There are times when you may nurture your staff (Coach) and others when you may be more playful (Friend) or inspirational (Compass). The book *The One Minute Manager* teaches the principle that Boss and Coach are generally brief: make criticism specific to one event and make it short. Likewise, make compliments specific and brief too. Avoid flattery and dramas. If you remain in Adult, you may well find problematic staff improve. Otherwise, a clear disciplinary process will need to be followed. When the drama stops, sometimes these people simply leave of their own accord.

## Drivers

This is another concept from TA that is hugely helpful for leaders, and which maps well onto the archetypes. Drivers are patterns of behaviour programmed into us in childhood, which we then act out unconsciously as adults, and in doing so create problems for ourselves and others around us. Most people have at least one of these. They are:

Hurry Up
Be Perfect
Be Careful
Try Hard
Be Strong
Please People

The following section maps these TA drivers onto the archetypes and shadows. I have written them in a slightly extreme way to illustrate the points clearly.

The Express Train is a natural archetype for *Hurry Up* people. Such people love making things happen fast, but often have to pick up the pieces later. I am a Hurry Up, and although this gave me a healthy natural Express Train, it meant I made many mistakes. This made me develop a very loud Alarm Bell, when I could have better anticipated trouble using my Architect more (producing a gentler ring of the Bell). Hurry Up people can also have a large Steamroller, which can cause significant damage to an organisation. You can't Hurry Up out of everything. The 'Hurry Up' person needs to develop a good Architect and listen to the Alarm Bell if things are going too fast.

By contrast, the Express Train is anathema for *Be Perfect* people – they prefer the Architect and the Alarm Bell: don't launch anything until it is perfect. However, the Second Life story, quoted in the section on the Express Train in Chapter 3, shows the problem with this type of thinking. A better Express Train would have given the team the motivation to get a beta version of the product in front of potential users, rather than endlessly strive after pre-launch perfection.

Be Perfect is also a key feature of professional training, from engineers to solicitors. However, even professions rely on mistakes from the past, fixed by centuries of experience within those professions.

Sadly, in business, the time that perfection takes will mean that the business will become too slow to survive. Be Perfect leaders will tend to have a large Tinkerer and cause ossification of an organisation, where backlogs will begin to drown departments. During this time, a true problem will emerge that requires urgent attention. The Be Perfect leader will be overwhelmed by the backlog which they believe still needs to be dealt with perfectly; they will ignore the Alarm Bell and not spot this urgent situation.

The *Be Careful* person dislikes both the Express Train and the Architect. For them it is all about the Alarm Bell. Using ever more complex avoidance strategies, fearful of investment in potentially risky new products or processes as well as of moving fast, the Be Careful spends much of their time trying to prevent themselves from going into Headless Chicken. Smaller professional partnerships often vote for a Be Careful leader who will exercise good stewardship but will keep the peace by not changing things or challenging their other partners.

These partnerships tend to become prime take-over targets, as the lack of dynamism and creativity allows their competitors to grow and eventually devour them. The Be Careful needs to understand that without the Express Train and a busy Architect, they are actually putting their organisation in great danger.

The *Try Hard* person never actually completes things – they are too busy trying to do them (Eric Berne, who created TA, used an image from Greek mythology: Sisyphus was condemned by the gods to push a stone up a hill, but when he got near the top it would always roll down to the bottom again). Try Hard leaders are in a constant state of stress. Believing that 'a leader's job is never done', they overwhelm themselves with work and create overly complex projects that stay too long in the design phase (classic Tinkerer). Even when their team have come up with a coherent plan, they will have had all sorts of new ideas and want changes. This causes frustration among the team and a sense that 'the goalposts are always moving.'

The *Be Strong* person tends to value the Boss and the Express Train, but also the Steamroller. Their motto is 'Just make it happen and tough it out'. They ignore the Alarm Bell and are inflexible when it comes to changing established processes (in other words, not enough Architect). The Be Strong leader needs to value work on processes. They will also lack Coach, feeling that people shouldn't be ruled by emotions, and that if they are ruled by emotions they are weak and inferior.

The opposite of Be Strong is *Please People*. With a hair-trigger Alarm Bell if anyone gets upset, the people pleasing leader will tend to bend the rules and make the business less efficient to unreasonably pander to the needs of a few precious individuals. There is a challenging balance in business between catering to the needs of the workforce and delivering business outcomes. When the pendulum swings too far, a culture of preciousness can emerge, and in a competitive world this culture will simply not last. The Please People leader will then have destroyed the organisation, not really pleasing any one.

Being aware of which of these drivers you have is essential, so that you can make adjustments. Having a good balance of the three operations and finance archetypes – Architect, Express Train and Alarm Bell – is the solution to most of the personality issues raised by Drivers.

## NLP

NLP provides a way for people who didn't study psychology to have a rapid and practical way of learning the subject along with coaching and leadership skills. It helped transform my business acumen.

NLP is not a system or a world view. It is a set of concepts and personal development tools. Since its creation in the 1970s by John Grinder and Richard Bandler at the University of California Santa Cruz (UCSC), NLP has grown into a global psychological movement. NLP principles and techniques are often the basis behind books and courses on leadership, influencing, negotiations and presentation skills. The field has been greatly enhanced by Robert Dilts who has developed much of the modern NLP toolkit, including cutting edge work on leadership and coaching. Other remarkable contributors include Judith Delozier, Stephen Gilligan and Steve and Connierae Andreas.

The letters NLP stand for Neuro-Linguistic Programming. Breaking this name down:

- *Neuro* – NLP has to do with the brain and with other neurological systems in the body. Our brain can be compared to the 'hardware' inside a computer.
- *Linguistic* – This is then the 'software' that runs our brain. What is fascinating is how as children we learn basic language skills (software), and this actually rewires our 'hardware' and makes it perform better. This in turn enables us to understand increasingly complex ideas, which continues to rewire our hardware in more advanced ways. This virtuous circle means that by the age of six, we are far more sophisticated than any other mammal on this planet – language is a miracle. However, NLP is not just about language; much of NLP is about *other* ways in which we process information, using the five senses and things like gestures and body language – also forms of communication that rewire our hardware.
- *Programming* – The downside to our language acquisition is that many of our negative repeated thoughts, reactions, beliefs, patterns of behaviour are programmed into our brains and now run there outside our conscious awareness. We may pick them up in early childhood or learn them through generalising negative experiences. NLP is essentially a way of identifying these unhelpful programmes, and replacing them with new, more helpful ones.

Here is an example of using a tool from NLP called the 'Meta Model', which is designed to spot the misleading language people use in expressing negative beliefs, but which can also be very useful to spot if someone else is trying to mislead you. A lawyer acting for a company with whom we were having a financial dispute pointed out that an email showed that our 'Mr A' understood one principle, and went on to say that this meant that Mr A also understood another principle, too. My NLP 'nose' spotted the potentially dubious word 'meant'. This is called a 'Complex Equivalence': when someone asserts that 'x means y', it might be true, or it might not be, but the link is tenuous and not *necessarily* true. The elevated and smug tone of voice this lawyer used also alerted my Fox. I dug out the email, challenged the logic of the assertion, and they gave in.

I cover the Meta Model along with many other useful business approaches from NLP in my book *How to Coach with NLP*.

I know NLP has not been without its critics. It has sometimes been associated with inappropriate selling techniques. However, the vast majority of NLP has been used in a positive way by individuals keen to improve their own lives and the lives of others around them. It also provides an excellent set of tools to equip the modern leader with the deeper psychological approaches that can give them an edge. As the famous English academic, Gregory Bateson, said, it can help you discover 'the difference which makes a difference'.

## The NLP Matrix Coach

This is more powerful version of the Matrix Coach discussed in Chapter 5. It essentially does the same – invites you to visit each archetype in turn and let it have its say. However, it uses an NLP technique called *anchoring*. It is a deeper process and it takes longer, especially the first time you use it, thereafter, it soon becomes intuitive.

Anchoring is a deliberate way of setting something up so you can use it later to change your state of mind automatically. A simple example is putting a photo on your desk (or phone), or putting on some music that inspires or excites you. There are dozens of little rituals we do to help us change our state. The science behind this comes from Ivan Pavlov, who found that ringing a bell at the time of feeding a hungry dog meant that the dog began to salivate when they heard the bell again, even if no food were present. The dog had associated the sound of the bell with the food. Likewise, we can associate a physical sensation (such as a touch on one of our knuckles) with a desired state we wish to enter.

I will guide you through this exercise at www.nlpschool.com/meditate.

## Part one: setting it up

This first section you only need to do once. It is simply a way of experiencing each archetype without any particular agenda. Once you have done this, you can use Part 2 frequently to explore decisions or strategic issues that are a challenge to you.

Begin by gently clenching your fist, so your four knuckles stand out. You will be anchoring to these four knuckles (if that seems odd, please hold any confusion and read on).

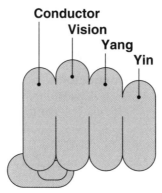

1   The first archetype you need to access is that of the **Conductor**. Allow yourself to simply relax and settle. The Conductor is about detachment and cool – so allow yourself to simply accept how you are right now. You don't need to change anything and you can let go of a need to think about

the future or the past. Just allow your attention to sink into your body, where you can notice yourself breathe. When you have a strong sense of being present and relaxed, press the knuckle on your *index* finger until the feeling starts to fade. Pause for a few moments and then press the knuckle again. You should find that the sense of presence and relaxation lightly returns. If it does not, repeat the exercise a few times until it does. You have now anchored this state of mind to that knuckle.

2    Next, anchor a sense of **Vision** on your middle finger knuckle. Allow your imagination to pass through recollections of having a sense of destiny, imagination and optimism. A feeling that anything is possible … Allow your eyes to look upward towards an imagined future, and just get this sense. Allow this energy to be uncensored. When you have this sense strongly, press the knuckle on your *middle* finger until the feeling starts to fade. Pause briefly and then press the knuckle again. You should find that the 'anything is possible' feeling lightly returns. If it does not, repeat the exercise a few times until it does. You have now anchored this state of mind to that knuckle.

3    Next, anchor **Yang**, on your ring finger knuckle. Allow your imagination and memory to create or recall sensations of strength and resolve. Remember times when you were grounded and still. Remember times when you were able to act and assert boundaries. When you have a strong sense of being strong and 'at cause', press the knuckle on your *ring* finger until the feeling starts to fade. Test in the same way by pressing the knuckle again.

4    Finally anchor **Yin** on your little finger knuckle. Allow your imagination to summon up a sense of connection both to yourself and to others. A genuine caring for yourself and others; bring yourself to mind and bring a platonic close friend to mind too. Enjoy a sense of caring. See if you can extend this sense of well-wishing to others, while retaining this positive feeling of sensitivity. When you have a strong sense of this feeling, press the knuckle on your *little* finger until the feeling starts to fade. Pause and then press the knuckle again.

**Part two: how to use your NLP Matrix Coach**

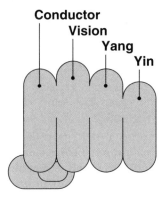

1 Bring to mind the project or decision you are thinking about.

2 Press the Conductor knuckle. Allow yourself to relax and concentrate on your breathing. You can even imagine yourself standing outside yourself, watching. When you feel sufficiently relaxed and detached, move on to the next step.

3 Explore the Leadership row. Consider your issue from the perspective of the Compass (middle finger), Boss (ring finger) and then Coach (little finger knuckle). Take your time on each. Which one brings you new information?

4 Repeat with the Operations/Finance row. Likewise, consider your issue from the perspective of the Architect (middle), Express Train (ring) and Alarm Bell (little). Which one brings you new information?

5 Repeat with the Sales/Marketing row. Again, consider your issue from the perspective of the Radar (middle finger), Fox (little finger) and Friend (ring finger). Which one brings you new information?

6 Return to the Conductor knuckle. Did one or more of the archetypes provide you with something important to consider? If so, revisit the relevant knuckle. Also notice if you felt more emotional on any knuckle. Did one or more of the shadows come up? Work out what is the positive motivation behind any shadow and what positive action you need to take to honour that motivation. Allow that positive motivation to come from one of the archetypes instead. For instance, the Bully may encourage you to express your own needs with a firm, but steady, Boss energy.

7 Are you now ready to take a decision or a next step? While you are on the Conductor knuckle, make sure it 'agrees' with this. If it does, trust it.

8 If you still feel unsure of a course of action, accept this. Sometimes the best thing to do is to do nothing. The Conductor is generally willing to buy some time out to think and to allow the various shadows that can play out in the drama of business to settle within yourself.

Experiment with this process so it works best for you. The principle behind it is that:

1 Each archetype has its say, its 'day in court'.

2 The archetypes that will be of most use in sorting out the issue are discovered, so that the 'best' and least biased path to progress is identified.

3 The Conductor is the final arbiter.

# Index

# Taylor & Francis eBooks

## Helping you to choose the right eBooks for your Library

Add Routledge titles to your library's digital collection today. Taylor and Francis ebooks contains over 50,000 titles in the Humanities, Social Sciences, Behavioural Sciences, Built Environment and Law.

**Choose from a range of subject packages or create your own!**

**Benefits for you**

>> Free MARC records
>> COUNTER-compliant usage statistics
>> Flexible purchase and pricing options
>> All titles DRM-free.

**Benefits for your user**

>> Off-site, anytime access via Athens or referring URL
>> Print or copy pages or chapters
>> Full content search
>> Bookmark, highlight and annotate text
>> Access to thousands of pages of quality research at the click of a button.

REQUEST YOUR **FREE** INSTITUTIONAL TRIAL TODAY | **Free Trials Available** We offer free trials to qualifying academic, corporate and government customers.

## eCollections – Choose from over 30 subject eCollections, including:

| | |
|---|---|
| Archaeology | Language Learning |
| Architecture | Law |
| Asian Studies | Literature |
| Business & Management | Media & Communication |
| Classical Studies | Middle East Studies |
| Construction | Music |
| Creative & Media Arts | Philosophy |
| Criminology & Criminal Justice | Planning |
| Economics | Politics |
| Education | Psychology & Mental Health |
| Energy | Religion |
| Engineering | Security |
| English Language & Linguistics | Social Work |
| Environment & Sustainability | Sociology |
| Geography | Sport |
| Health Studies | Theatre & Performance |
| History | Tourism, Hospitality & Events |

For more information, pricing enquiries or to order a free trial, please contact your local sales team:
**www.tandfebooks.com/page/sales**

 **Routledge** Taylor & Francis Group | The home of Routledge books | **www.tandfebooks.com**